Migrants & Stowaways

Migrants & Stowaways

AN ANTHOLOGY OF JOURNEYS

EDITED BY EMILY DZIUBAN
WITH KRISTIN ROBERTSON

A publication of the Knoxville Writers' Guild
KNOXVILLE, TENNESSEE

Printed in USA by Thomson-Shore

THE KNOXVILLE WRITERS' GUILD
P.O. Box 10326
Knoxville, TN 37939-0326
www.knoxvillewritersguild.org

COVER ART: *My Fiftieth Year* by Melynda Whetsel
Suitcase photograph by Lisa Horstman

Book design by Lisa Horstman
www.lisahorstman.com

CONTENTS

Contents

STONES' THROWS

Contents

THE METAPHORS

Contents

INTRODUCTION

Fly to Costa Rica. Hire a tourist bus to drive you to the Eco-Lodge near Coter Lake. Don't fall asleep on the way. Watch out the window for the Catholic churches, central parks, bars, primary schools and soccer fields that exist in every Costa Rican town no matter how small. Check in. Hire a guide. Begin on the path embedded in the Three Days Plant. You'll know it because it flowers all year long with bright purple blooms for tomorrow, faded white for today, and wilted brown for yesterday. On the path, don't touch anything. Don't steady yourself with a hand on a nearby tree. Don't reach out for an impossibly beautiful bud. You are in the rainforest where poison abounds.

After thirty minutes of walking, approach a dark, smoky hut belonging to an indigenous tribe. Ball your right fist and gently tap it on the left shoulders of the men in organic skirts who greet you. Say "Capi, Capi." They'll do the same. Feel stupid. Listen to a translated explanation of their Iguana farming and the natural diet that keeps them alive for at least ninety years apiece. See no women. Wonder where the women are but don't ask. Buy at least one hundred guilty dollars in masks, rain sticks, bowls, drums and necklaces. As you leave, hear this translated from Maleku to Spanish to English: "Thank you for coming to the rainforest to see us. Please tell others that there are people called Maleku who still live in the rainforest and who only use what the rainforest gives them." When you arrive home, do as the man says.

The poets, writers and artists collected in this anthology have done as the man says. They may not have gone to the Costa Rican rainforest but they have journeyed. Some have simply imagined journeys. All know, however, that the most important part is coming home and telling the tale.

When the board of the Knoxville Writers' Guild met to select a theme for their sixth anthology, I was still the kind of member who came late to readings, sat in the back, and snuck out early before anyone tried to mingle with me. By the time the Guild solicited for editors, I had watched them from my wallpaper perspective enough to know they were a friendly, intelligent bunch genuinely interested in good writing. I took the editor's post without a clue as to the book's subject. I then recruited Kristin Robertson to help me, mostly by misleading her regarding the amount of work required. Together we learned the theme: Journeys.

Great! World trips! Far off places! We figured research in the form of cappuccinos at Western European street cafés was in order. But over the course of the next several months, we started to see journeys in everything we did. Teach a class: journey. Teach a class poorly: difficult journey. Drive to Kroger: journey. Take the dogs around the block: journey. Understand a new philosophical concept: journey. Edit a book: journey. Remember who said that there are only two plots in fiction, someone takes a trip and a stranger comes to town: journey cubed. These were dark days.

Our editorial quagmire expanded as we removed ourselves from the position of protagonists and considered the journeys that frame history. We went: out of the Garden, up to Mt. Olympus to steal fire, out of Africa, into Troy via a hollow horse, across the Bering Straight, across the Atlantic with disastrously good intentions, down the Mississippi on a raft with a runaway, out to California for gold then just for work, down with the Titanic and up to the moon. Kristin and I lived the storied, journeyed lives of Queen Elizabeth, Albert Einstein, Mohammad, and Santa Claus.

Then we started to read. Great piles of inspiring manuscripts naturally sorted themselves into the three kinds of journeys that seem to change us all. In the *Far From East Tennessee* section, gentle reader, you will find stories and poems that will make you want to stick pins in a wall map. Mark DeKay contemplates how the architecture of Gandhi's home, which he traveled to see first hand, reveals what lacks in our own conceptions of community. Curt Rode and Margaret Pennycook both provide poetic examinations of the journey our bodies take after we pass from them. Jo Ann Pantanizopoulos invites us to the baptism before her Grecian wedding.

Stones' Throws honors our explorations of our own backyards, where some of our most important realizations are made. The "Co-Pilots" of Susanna Greenberg's story survey a handful of Southern states from the perspective of Northerners. Debra A. Poole and Steve Sparks call our attention to rivers, bodies of water that both travel extensively and never go anywhere. Don Williams writes of a lawyer who must make a realization of the heart before he can pursue the woman who has left town.

Finally, *The Metaphors* collects pieces in which the biggest journeys happen within characters' minds regardless of whether their bodies move. One of the most important journeys of Jeanne McDonald's life is one she cannot remember. Jerry Peterson and Judy DiGregorio create characters, fictional or no, who must accept the realities of their physical beings in order to progress. Most of all, poets dominate this section, exploring image after image after image of the small realizations that define lifetimes.

Without question, I too should wax poetic about the journey you are about to take reading this book. I've drawn the map, advised you of the weather and am even now closing the clasp on your suitcase. Your journey starts with the turn of the page.

—*Emily Dziuban*

CROSSROADS: DOWNTOWN
by Catie Tappan

$\mathcal{A}$CKNOWLEDGMENTS

$\mathcal{H}$ardly any traveler arrives at her destination without help. Even those who would climb a mountain alone seek advice from those who climbed before. They register with the ranger station in case of avalanche. They ask the clerk at the supply store which energy gel will sustain them longer. For Kristin and I, the first source of help came from the board of the Knoxville Writers' Guild, as well as its general membership, who published this book. The Guild is a non-profit that serves and encourages East Tennessee Writers of all skill levels. On the Guild's behalf, we also thank the following for their financial and additional support:

Two Anonymous Friends

The Clayton Family Foundation

The College of Arts and Sciences of the University of Tennessee, Knoxville

Judy DiGregorio

The East Tennessee Foundation

The English Department of the University of Tennessee, Knoxville

Dennis McCarthy

Mr. K's Used Books and CDs in Oak Ridge and Johnson City

NDI Group, Inc.

Jim and Teri Rooney

Arthur Stewart

Lewis Willis

Along the way, many individuals helped us stay the course, including Jeannette Brown who was a godsend of advice and Flossie McNabb who provided inspiration. Melynda Whetsel created an unbelievably inspirational collage and allowed us to use it for far below its worth. Heather Robertson donated her time and professional expertise. The English Department at the University of Tennessee, particularly Marilyn Kallet, Michael Knight, Art Smith, Allen Wier, Judith Welch and John Zomchick, provides support and resources for many of the writers in this book, including the editors. Julie Auer, Marybeth Boyanton and Matt Forsythe reviewed the manuscript with care. J. Brian Long, Rip Lydick, Kay Newton and Patricia Waters spent many hours reading line by line. Pamela Schoenewaldt was a touchstone of support for better than a year. Brian Griffin offered sage advice and made overtures on our behalf. Jo Angela Edwins listened with patience to things no one should have to hear. Lisa Horstman dazzled us with design. Laura Still answered myriad questions and ran myriad errands. Nicole Underwood and Judy DiGregorio created a publicity storm. The contributors made this book unlike any other.

Emily personally thanks Kim Stone whose loving kindness has supported this project from the day it was conceived until well after this acknowledgement will be read. Emily is also grateful to the families that love her no matter what journeys she embarks on: the Dziubans scattered in Florida and the Connellys and Aunt Jackie, the Nettleses, and the Hugheses scattered in South Carolina.

Kristin personally thanks her family for always asking "how's the book coming?" and Brian Goddard for loving and supporting a writer.

If anything in this volume requires blame, look not to this list of generous and intelligent people.

MY FIFTIETH YEAR
by Melynda Whetsel

ABOUT THE COVER ART

If you close this book and gaze at the cover, you will likely find yourself sinking into the complexity of the images, absorbing the rich textures, the layered golds and browns, and drifting away on a journey through leaves, past dinosaurs, on the wings of those archetypal migrants, the butterflies. To us, the cover art is, in a word, *glorious*.

And we happened upon it by luck. Emily and I knew that we wanted to invite a regional artist to donate her talent and connote our vision. We wandered through galleries, browsed watercolors and sketches, and while we liked a number of suitable pieces, we trusted our impulses that we had yet to find the perfect work. We kept the anthology uncovered and our fingers crossed.

Then, one weekend my aunt showed me a postcard from an art show in Knoxville. The collage on the front captivated and intrigued me. Emily and I began brainstorming with it in front of us. All of a sudden we had a frame, a suitcase, if you will, which we felt could contain the contents of this book.

The cover art captures both the literal and metaphorical journey, incorporating passages of time, physical aging, birth, death, and, of course, sojourns through real and mythical lands and seas. From the collage we derived the title, *Migrants and Stowaways*. The nautical compass marks our travels, encourages us to stow away and relish the treasures, the spilled bounty of the lives shared here.

The title of the collage, *My Fiftieth Year*, celebrates the life experiences of one of East Tennessee's most accomplished artists. Melynda Whetsel is not only a local mainstay in the Knoxville artistic community, frequently hosting art shows and renovating Victorian homes in the eclectic Fourth and Gill historic district, but she is also a top art and art history educator.

When we met with Whetsel, we became even more convinced that her artwork was the best choice for this collection of poetry and prose. The process of creating the collage, the layering of the mixed media, beginning with magazine clippings of old china plates, seemed to us to be the perfect symbol of the journey. Here, Whetsel describes her masterpiece:

> *Life, like art, is composed of layers. Units of time and the experiences each hold are laid one upon the other. Images ripple to the surface, others fade, some are buried. The quality of each—life and art—is dependent upon balance. The fulcrum, often evasive, measures human frailty against strength, love against hate, feminine from masculine, right from wrong, fat from lean, holding on or letting go, birth against death just as surely as it weighs line from shape or lights against darks. When these battles are completed and the canvas is laid out before us, we see and reflect and possibly understand. And then we begin again.*

We suspect that you will not quickly forget the cover of this anthology; we hope it stays with you in your mind and on your coffee table. Each time you glance at it, you will notice something new—embark on a brief journey—and dive into the book for traverses and time well spent. We could all use this passport for a clean getaway.

—*Kristin Robertson*

Under the
Jackson Street
Bridge 1
by David Habercom

JUDY AT THE *LOUVRE*
by Kim Stone

Far from East Tennessee

Pamela Schoenewaldt

ONE LAST ESPRESSO

$\mathcal{M}$y mother died in Texas just before noon. The end came faster than anyone expected, and since I lived in Italy, I wasn't there with her. But she came to see me late that night and we drank coffee together, not big, companionable American mugs, just straight shots of espresso. Still, we nearly had our miracle.

Her chest pain started late last summer, a massive tumor on the lung eating towards the heart. "The worst I've seen in twenty years," the oncologist told my father, but they started chemo anyway; it was something to do. On the phone I heard her voice grow weaker through the fall, resenting everything, furious with her doctor: the diagnosis must be wrong or else the treatment wasn't working; he was "letting" more new tumors grow. When I said I'd take a leave of absence and come back home, she refused: "Not now when the doctor's got me down like this. Come in the spring when I'm back to normal." To calm her, I agreed, but planned to go at Christmas. In the calls that followed, always shorter and more resentful, she never once conceded she was dying or said she loved me. I knew all about the seven stages to a peaceful death, how they start with anger, blame, denial. But they were her natural states. She didn't get beyond them.

Nor did I. Sometimes I daydreamed the chemo really could be working and she'd be healed, enlightened and repentant. Failing that, in Texas I'd make rice pudding like she made when I was small, before the bad times started. If rice pudding didn't cure her, at least we'd be reconciled. I'd sit by the bed and she'd eat slowly—even in my fantasies, I

2

couldn't picture feeding her—and all our endemic bitterness would simply fade away. I'd say, "I know you tried, Mom," and she'd reply, "I always loved you, even when I drank." I'd forgive her generously and we'd have our Christmas miracle, just like in the movies.

Instead she died December 21st, the day before my ticket home. The tumor had suddenly gone wild, bursting into her lungs and filling them with blood. By the time my father reached me on the phone, the men from the crematorium had taken her away.

"I should have come before, no matter what she said," I told my father over and over until he, to comfort me, said let me tell you how it was: hair all gone and face swollen up around sunken raisin-eyes, chest like raw meat from the radiation, shunts all over and tubes and catheters, groggy, bitter, cursing. Why remember her that way?

"Go to bed and get some sleep," he said. "You've got a long flight tomorrow. I'll see you at the airport and we'll talk before the funeral." But it wasn't him I needed.

I hung up and wandered through our apartment, feeling half-dead myself, as if my feet made no impression on the floor. My husband watched in silence, then asked if I wanted chamomile tea or else a whiskey, "like in American films." I sat, stood and started wandering again. Seeing his worried face, I said perhaps I'd try to sleep. It was scarcely ten o'clock, but he said he was tired himself and came to bed with me. I lay still, thinking of Texas. By now the men from the crematorium had finished their work.

I woke after midnight in the winter dark. There was someone in the house, a silent presence just arrived, not a stranger or a thief. I'd read how the spirit briefly visits its people before the final passing. Besides, my mother had never seen where I live in Italy. She disliked traveling, and in truth, my invitations had not been pressing.

I felt doors soundlessly open and close as someone peered into our rooms with exactly her insistent, relentless curiosity for materials and dimensions: is this metal or wood? How wide is the window? Hall? Closet? Never schooled, my mother had designed houses, dogged and bullied her contractors, found supplies they swore didn't exist, pushed hard on standards and deadlines; incredibly, they ended friends. One still keeps her picture on his desk. I never did.

After the kitchen, living room and bathroom, she examined our laundry room and study. I pushed close to my husband and he held me in his sleep. Perhaps now she'd notice, although she never had before, how after all the bad years and bad men, at last I'd found peace. Perhaps she'd be happy for me. I felt her move toward the bedroom, glance in and notice us together, but then translucent glass panels in our door distracted her. She examined the brass handles, the storage closet and its similar handles, then drifted down the hall. I slipped out of bed, dressed, and found her in the kitchen, studying my cabinets.

As always, she skipped the salutations and her eyes slid past me as she talked. "Oh, you're up. Where's the American coffee?" Actually she wanted Brim, her customary brand of de-caf. I had only espresso. I was wrong again and insufficient.

"Does caffeine really matter now?" I asked peevishly. I pictured her collection of Brim jars: tall, brown-lidded, rows on rows carefully labeled for buttons, beads, brushes, leather tools and calligraphy pens, supplies for crafts projects cleverly started but soon abandoned. I closed the kitchen door and started grinding coffee.

Kitchen light shone on her hair, the rich red brown of before the chemotherapy. Was it relief or inconvenience to come back to her own well body? "Your doors have handles instead of knobs," she observed suddenly. I gripped the grinder.

"Italian doors have handles."

"*All* of them? *Nobody* has knobs?"

"I don't know, Mom. I haven't checked."

She studied our kitchen door, playing with the handle. "They're easier than knobs for arthritics. Is there a lot of arthritis in Italy?"

"Mom, I don't know." I filled the espresso maker, stamping down the coffee hard.

"And those panels in the doors give light, but isn't privacy an issue here?"

"I guess not."

"Well," she mused, "anyway, you don't have kids. You're still trying?"

I nodded. She knew we were. "Instant would be fine," she announced.

"We only have espresso."

"Well, then I'll take mine with cream. You do have cream?" I had no cream and no all-night convenience store around the corner. I was prepared to defend the Italian mercantile system when she asked what I had to eat. I got out biscotti, nuts and chocolate. She was never fat but always hid secret stores of snacks. Later she hid liquor. Did she remember how that started?

For years she put two martini glasses in the freezer at 5:30 every weekday evening. When my father came home they had one drink each in frosted glasses with olives or tiny pickled onions and chatted about the day. Eventually he must have noticed that only his glass was frosted and only his drink garnished. Hers was gin, straight up. She started using juice, then water glasses, not our delicate martini cones. Nights were turning harsh. Then came whole ugly days, at first so carefully planned that no one but the family noticed them. But soon her planning slipped. The problem was public now: at Christmas parties, my sister's graduation or my first wedding. I flew home once on a bad day. She threw a lamp at me that shattered at my feet. I told my father, "If there's no flight out tonight, take me to a bus. I'll come back when she apologizes."

My father brought me to the station. I knew she'd sweep up the shards in the morning, buy another lamp and never mention the episode or ever apologize. But churning with anger and resentment, I would never forget it. Years passed. My father entrenched and endured; my younger sister Becky slipped home on the good days and steadily ignored the rest. But I made my life apart, first in other cities and then another country. On every move the shards came with me. With his every kindness my new husband pleaded: couldn't you just put the past aside? He knew I tried.

Suddenly, with no more comment than when it started, the drinking simply ceased—no AA, no enlightenment or apology, all the broken things just ignored. She smoked much more, but as she constantly reminded us, she only hurt herself. You know, a doctor told me once, your mother may truly not remember the things she did to you; isn't it enough that she's dry? It wasn't, not for me. I wanted remorse and penance. I wanted: "I in whom your bones were knitted, I have always loved you." How else could I know I was loveable?

The espresso was steaming. I cut some cheese and took out more biscotti.

She helped me set the table with cloth napkins, plates and little spoons. For the moment our wariness fell away and we had that secret time you sometimes find in kitchens when everyone else is sleeping, like finding a new room in your own house. We spoke of the week they found the shadow in her lung; she made a birthday party for my little niece. She had done what she could for us. Why tally offenses like a miser counting coins? Just let it go, and in the space left free, surely our souls would meet. I felt a tiny cracking in my chest.

"I'm happy now with my husband," I said finally.

"It took awhile, didn't it, to find a good one? But I'm glad for you, dear." She rearranged the cheese. "How are mortgage rates in Italy? Couldn't you buy a place instead of rent?" I said the rates were high, and anyway we might move north. She studied our kitchen and observed the layout was efficient. "Small, though."

She noted our small refrigerator and lack of window over the sink. First I played with biscotti crumbs and then just closed my eyes. Questions drummed in the dark: Mom, did you know you'd die? Weren't you afraid? What did you think about in the downstairs bedroom, where first there were magazines, then pills for nausea, then oxygen tanks, a walker, bedpans, catheters, all the heralds of inexorable decay? Waiting for sleep, how far back did your thoughts run? Did you find peace? I opened my eyes. "Mom—"

"The doctor should have changed the treatment," she was saying. "He *saw* the tumor growing." I nodded, remembering what the doctor had said about her case. "Because if he'd done that, I might have gotten better."

"Maybe. Where are you going now? Have you seen Becky?"

"I'm going in order and you're the oldest. It's only fair." I remembered "fair," the consolation prize when she couldn't give us love. "And besides, I've never been to Italy. You didn't ask me to the wedding."

"We did. You didn't come."

"Nobody goes to Italy in November. Why not in the spring, in Tuscany or someplace nice?" We were at it again. Our voices rose and then fell silent. She took another biscotti and pushed the plate to me. I shook my head. We heard my husband stir. "I'm glad to see you doing well," she said.

"Was it hard getting here?"

"No, just long. I found it right away, you sent us pictures, remember those little books?" Yes, our little books of photographs, I wrote captions and my husband made the covers.

She got up suddenly, washed the dishes, dried and put them away. In the morning there'd be no sign. She came to my chair and kissed me lightly on the hair; she didn't smell of cigarettes. "You know I quit," she said proudly, "as soon as I got the diagnosis."

"Mom, please don't go! Stay with me!"

But she was across the kitchen, leaning against the sink. "It's all right, honey, it's over. Remember I made you rice pudding. You knew I loved you," she said quickly, tripping through the words. "The rest of it was my own business."

"Not just yours. All those years—"

"Mine. My business, my problems. You had your own." I sat in silence as sharp things crumbled in my heart. My own business? She wet a sponge and wiped our marble counter clean and clear as a midnight lake, reflecting the moon of our ceiling lamp but not her quiet face. She had never loved cooking, but I remembered how peaceful her kitchen always was, even in the bad years, all the clamor of pots and appliances neatly stowed away. Meanwhile I'd floundered in distant cities, waking in strange places, using other people's kitchenettes, cutting out when trouble started.

"There," she said. "That's done."

"You're leaving?"

She nodded. "You have a lovely apartment, the layout, everything. Someday you'll have a house, maybe kids, why not?" I nodded slowly. Cool night air fanned me as if from an open window. "Go back to your husband now," my mother said. "He'll be waking soon and missing you." So I couldn't see her go. When I stopped at the kitchen door, she waved me away.

Lying in bed, I felt her pass across our living room. She must have left by the balcony, crossing the fields between our house and the sea. Perhaps they reminded her of Texas, where there's green even in the wintertime. Our bed was warm. When I knew she'd gone, I fell asleep easily and woke up crying in the morning.◆

IN SHANGHAI

noodles slither
on plates of rice

to the native tasters
they swim throats venomless

satiate bodies
skipping of saffron
that airs Shanghai cafes

the king cobras of noodles
fan evergreen flavours to the city

in which I'm tourist
starving to translate its taste

Jane Sasser

On the Bright Angel Trail

Sliding over the crust of ice,
I am grateful for the first time
for the blessings of manure,
for the smelly traction
left by trains of mules.
Far down the canyon walls,
warm morning light
eases its way up
this frozen path. In overhangs
sometimes we glimpse red pictographs:
swollen horses dance across
yellow rock, ancient meanings lost.

Now ice gives way to mud,
to red dust, the sun
parching us too. Reckless,
we gulp whole gallons
of water, smooth and clean
down the throat like a blessing,
turning in our minds the images
of settlers who survived
this bold, half-barren land.
Above us vermilion walls
hold like thick columns
a heavy blue sky. Ravens
float, soundless, wings buoyed

on puffs of rising heat.
The rhythm of our feet
trudging forward, down,
moves us past eons of rock.

Indian Gardens bloom,
green oasis, where mule deer
glide through cottonwood shadows,
creek water sings a path
down to Bright Angel Camp.
We cross the broad plateau,
our steps white curls of dust
winding through purple cacti
to the sharp cliff edge. Far below,
the exultant Colorado,
chocolate river of debris,
whispers up to us,
deceptively hushed,
like old memories.

We loop back the way we came.
Walking now seems separate:
our minds float away,
leaving our bodies below
like old cicada shells. But
heat, thirst, movement
bring us always back
to who we are. We shuffle
past rock, green, purple, red,
miles sifting like flour
under our churning boots.
Mid-afternoon brings shade,
then icy mud, a slushy mix
of red clay and green manure.
We celebrate at the canyon rim,
achievement rarely so tangible.

As evening creeps in, the wind
mourns like coyote calls,
and we lean over the canyon wall,
watching, far in the gorge below,
twinkling flashlights bob
like stars on the Bright Angel Trail.

Julie Auer

A LETTER TO MABEL DODGE
BY _____

Dear Mrs. Luhan,

I want something, and I think you could help me. I wouldn't have dared to write such a storied patron of the arts as yourself when you were at your peak, and I probably would have shrunk from it when you were old. But I figure now, since you're dead, you don't get many calls. And to let you know I'm not looking for just any dead muse, and that I've done my homework, I won't tell you about myself at first. I'll tell you about you.

You were from Buffalo. You lived your epic life in Boston, Florence, Manhattan, and Taos, New Mexico. You were always rich, and you got on your first society high in Manhattan when you were in your teens. You married and had a son early, and your husband died in a hunting accident. So you found another husband, the architect named Dodge, who took you to Florence and the villa with the white turrets and tile rooftops, the Renaissance statuary and imported hothouse flowers.

You invited Gertrude Stein and Alice B. Toklas to your Florentine castle, away from the violence of World War I Paris, so Stein could write. I wonder if you heard any of their infamous rows, for no doubt they had them, because Alice felt threatened by you. You were Stein's kind of woman. She wrote one of her indecipherable short stories for you. We know it's about you because the words "Miss Dodge" appear in it over and over again. Other than that, nobody knows what the hell it's about. But you kept copies of it for posterity, handing them out as party favors for years.

When you left Dodge for the artist Maurice Sterne, you returned to New York. Just when things were heating up in postwar Paris for the Lost Generation, you found yourself in the dawn of Manhattan's Jazz Age. You met Georgia O'Keeffe, who was then running around with Alfred Stieglitz (as you would later run around with her sister, though on the sly). Heady days, the twenties: the champagne bottle of Manhattan was uncorked right around the time of Prohibition, and the bubbles poured out all the way into the black day in 1929 when your family lost much of its fortune.

You didn't give much of a damn, though, because by that time your spirit had blossomed in New Mexico. You arrived before the twenties hit their stride, in fact. You were ready for a simpler life, and a simpler man. Tony Luhan, a Taos Pueblo Indian, became the love of your life, but when you and Frida Kahlo crossed paths, there were rumors. Diego Rivera shrugged.

It may be, as Rivera once said, that women could take each other to a spiritual point that surpassed men's reach. But it was Luhan who took you to points beyond the reach of moneyed white guys from the right families. You were married for forty years until the hot day of your death in August 1962, high in the desert hills of Taos, where the air is thin and dry, the earth parched and serene, and the mountains seem to be watching us with something like the stoic, infuriating indifference of the eyes of God.

O'Keeffe settled in Abiquiu after spending a season with you in Taos, and she painted as though through the prism of divine sight. Willa Cather arrived reluctantly—she was a hard sell with her Nebraska earthiness and her New York airs—but she came anyway. While she worked on *Death Comes for the Archbishop*, the telling of a journey, a full journey of a soul, a body, a life, across the complex landscapes of time, place, and memory, she could have been writing a new book of the Bible for her prodigal patron.

I can't write biblical prose, and I'm more political than poetic, like John Reed and Emma Goldman, whose revolutionary hearts you won when they visited your Greenwich Village salon before your move to New Mexico, before Miss Goldman was tried for sedition and deported. You entertained radicals, though nobody knows if it was their politics or their unfettered passion for peace and justice that appealed to you most. I say it was passion, the juice of poetry that nourishes any just cause.

I say it was passion because you loved D.H. Lawrence best of all. You gave him a ranch near your home in return for his gift to you of the original manuscript of *Sons and Lovers*, and his wife, Frieda, had him buried there, in the crisp high hills of San Cristobal. He wrote of passion few men or women have in real life, muddled and strapped as real life is by standards of propriety. Every age has been enslaved to propriety, and every age's heroes are the ones who defy it. You were such a one, who lived a big life, whose progeny lives in the voices and images of the great artists of the twentieth century.

So where do I fit in? I don't pretend to rank among the likes of Lawrence, Cather, or O'Keeffe. I lack the gumption of Reed or Goldman. I'm a hack from a plain place and a vapid age, but I want to rise above it. I want to be a traitor to the false values of complacency and vanity. I want to sit in the sweaty, sun-baked studio of O'Keeffe, or in the lumpy, merry lap of Stein, right in Alice's glare. I want to feel the frigid Muscovite wind of Reed's last, hopeless stand. I want to see the sleeping beauty of the past come to new life in a world that doesn't confuse passion with pornography. I want to be one, small, infinitesimal spark in an awakening age.

Will you help me? ◆

RICHMOND, LATE '90s
by Bob R. Wilson

Terez Rose

TAKING THE GREEN LINE

"*Wild* and little-traveled" my guidebook had called the Auvergne, the heart of France's Massif Central, an area dotted with extinct volcanic peaks and craters spread out down a mountain chain. Our kind of France. My husband Peter and I had been intrepid, enthusiastic explorers in the region for a week one December. "So, what's the best way to get out of here?" Peter asked me that final chilly afternoon. I studied the map I'd procured at the local tourist office. It showed scenic routes marked in green lines. Blue lines meant major roads, like the *autoroute nationale* that would take us to Germany the following day. Green was fun; blue was serviceable, boring. We were leaving the rugged beauty of the Auvergne to visit relatives in the German flatlands. Peter's relatives. I needed my fun while I could get it. "How about completing the scenic circle from my map before getting on the autoroute?" I suggested.

"Sure. As long as it's a maintained road, nothing too steep or curvy. It'll be dark in just a few hours."

A series of squiggles on any map gives the savvy navigator an inkling that they most likely represented switchbacks, thus steep conditions. I could have spoken up and we'd probably have taken a blue road. Or I could have kept my mouth shut, we could check out some great scenery, and if it got too bad, I could play dumb, fall back on the excuse that my map didn't show elevations.

I kept my mouth shut.

THE FIRST TWO HOURS were ideal: good road conditions and fabulous scenery, the snow-capped mountains around us bathed in a golden, late-afternoon light. After a while however, I noticed the snow pack alongside the road accumulating. One inch became three and then six. I told myself the road wasn't really narrowing, but it was hard to pretend we weren't ascending in a rather steep manner. At the next junction, following green-line directions, we swung onto a smaller, less maintained road. Ten minutes later, the safe, rutted brown of the road was replaced by white. Clouds obscuring the setting sun painted an ominous hue over the wintery scene. "This is exactly what I wanted to avoid," Peter fretted, as we bumped over the packed snow.

"I'm just following directions from the map," I defended myself.

"I'm not questioning you, I'm just uncomfortable here." He reduced his speed. "But as long as it isn't icy, we'll be fine." Ten minutes later the dull white of the unplowed roads took on a pearly sheen. Ice. My muscles tensed. The silence in the car grew oppressive.

"I can handle it as long as it's not too steep," Peter said in a reassuring voice. But it didn't take a genius to work out the math: what goes up must come down, and we'd been steadily gaining elevation for some time now. When our car crested a hill fifteen minutes later, a terrifying panorama greeted us. In the fading light, majestic mountains and white hills crowded the view as far as the eye could see. It was the wild, spectacular scenery for which the region was famous, something you expected from the Alps, not from gentle south-central France. A "10% grade" sign was posted next to the road.

I couldn't speak. Peter's knuckles whitened as he slowed the car to a crawl. "Maybe it won't have that many curves," he practically whispered. You'd think by now he would have learned to keep his mouth shut. Z curves ahead, S curves, W curves, U curves, Q curves.

Why do I do this to myself? I wondered, not for the first time. Trips, culinary adventures, purchases, trying to get to the airport on time—it seemed my nature to want to always push the proverbial envelope. Only this time, the envelope might very well be pushed off the table, taking my husband and me with it.

We crept down the treacherous hills in first gear, both hardly daring to breathe for fear of somehow propelling the car off the edge of the narrow road. But it didn't stop the car from whooshing around the next curve. "I'm braking and nothing's happening," Peter said in a strained voice. For a few minutes (okay, four or five seconds) it was as if we were part of an audience watching a play, observing the car slide and idly wondering if there was going to be a crash.

But no crash this time. The little car finally skittered to an uneven stop, perilously close to a ditch. The interior of the car was quiet as we struggled to catch the breath our adrenaline had ripped out of us. A moment later, Peter squinted and peered through the windshield. "Do you see what I see?" he asked hesitantly.

A thin yellow beam of light in the darkening gloom soon revealed a lone bike rider, a small man bent over his mountain bike, trundling *up* the road we were afraid to drive down. We stared in open-mouthed surprise, watching as he passed by. He gave us brief nod and we nodded back, like polite strangers acknowledging each other at an English tea party. A moment later, he was gone. A baffled silence filled our car.

"We did see that, didn't we?" I asked carefully. We looked at each other for a moment before bursting into caws of laughter.

⚮

HAD IT NOT BEEN for the cyclist, the conflict could have easily degenerated into that timeless gender tango of who got us into this mess, who can't seem to get us out if it, the way safety, indeed, *honesty* was disregarded in the quest for adventure, how a real man wouldn't whine or lose control of the car, and why, by the way, can't you pick up your dirty socks? But it's hard to get too bent out of shape when a guy on a bicycle upstages your mountain drama. We laughed like idiots instead. It cleared the air better than a can of Lysol.

"I'm sorry I chose this road," I conceded a few minutes later.

"Sorry I almost drove us into a ditch."

After a few residual snickers, Peter started the car up and eased it back onto the road. Fifteen minutes later, the twinkling lights of a hamlet appeared. The road conditions eased, the hills leveled and soon we came upon an entrance to the *autoroute*, free of snow and ice, packed with drivers. The wimps. The ones who didn't need to take the green line. ◆

Brian Griffin

TENNESSEE BOY
ON THE PIAZZA SAN MARCO

a chisel in stone goes only so far:
same for opera, brush stroke, rose opening its satin eye.

on the Piazza San Marco they await the flood,
humor the child splashing among the cobblestones,

stone sinking, elegant, into mud: elegiac
smell of cafes, clatter of china

voices one with the hiss of espresso steam,
all the world still, settled as a sleeper's pulse:

how can they be so patient with the crawl of things?
sand-castle mansions tumor the hayfields of Tennessee,

the church-shorn headstones beside Chickamauga Lake
scoffing at themselves, at all notion of time

just as the winking moon draws light from the mountains
and sews them up in velvet, moonrise mocking all dawn.

near the dam roil rumors of towns submerged:
a village square, a courthouse, catfish and chub
at the City Cafe, old tires or refrigerators dumped
onto the steeples of churches, the roofs of barber shops

BRIAN GRIFFIN

weighted with mud and pebble like the backs of turtles
plodding the murky streets with a questioning turn of the head.

above, on the bass boats, we pretend to find peace
in the rituals of the Cherokee, lost now

but claimed by the eyeless imaginations of those desperate enough
to want it, want it all, the way a suited gondolier

once dove into the water of the Grand Canal
as though something besides murk awaited him there.

now on the Piazza San Marco, the waters puddle
beside the Campanile, and the stars of Galileo behind the clouds

shine as strong as the mosaic glittering in the cathedral vaults,
shining dark and lost, like something I know my father once said,

something I know my grandfather built,
something I know must stand strong beneath relentless water,

or inside me in the shifting blood of what I try to be,
patient, waiting, somewhere, somehow, in Tennessee.

PALINDROME

"A man, a plan, a canal: Panama"

*L*orenza Nuñez, my great-grand-
mother, was a witch. Just shy of five feet, she was close to eye-level with
the palms she read, and could trace the design of an entire life in the
chapped creases of an open hand.

Her daughter (my grandmother), Margarita Gomez, is a religious
fundamentalist. A petite but effective conduit for the righteous wrath
of God, she became a *testigo de Jehovah* (Jehovah's Witness) in the forties,
when she married my grandfather. Even today, at eighty, she will rap
forcefully on the doors of strangers, demanding they be saved.

My mother, Madeleine Swanstrom, is half witch, half religious fundamentalist, and sees no contradiction between the two. Get a few
drinks in her, and she will alternately quote the vengeful scripture of
the God of Abraham and hex the neighbor's dog for whizzing on her
front lawn in the suburban town of Thousand Oaks, California, where
she now lives.

Of the three worldviews that I have inherited from my mother, grandmother, and great-grandmother, I find my mother's eclectic and contradictory religion—her pick and choose approach to spirituality—the
most puzzling. She has no consistency. One day it's "Jesus Saves," and
the next its voodoo dolls and the evil eye. You can't have it both ways.

I like to tell myself that I believe in nothing. But despite my strong
claims to materialism, I have on my mantle a fat golden Buddha, a petite teakwood Buddha, a Jesus-on-wheels action figure, prayer beads,
joss candles, and yellow tissue paper to burn for the dead.

I would like to say that this is a collection of kitsch. These items are, after all, tacky and glittery, tawdry as ten-dollar whores. But I bristle at this comparison, even as I write it, because I have started to care for them. I dust the golden Buddha before leaving for school each day and make sure the teakwood Buddha faces the sunlight. There is nothing I have read that suggests that teakwood Buddhas require sunlight—his Holiness Siddhartha Gautama is not a fern—but something about his wide smile makes me want to put him in a sunbeam and make that smile grow wider. I keep my prayer beads clean and take Jesus-on-wheels out for a spin when he feels closed in. I light the joss candles when I am feeling blue, feeling grim, and burning yellow tissue paper has helped me get through the death of two close friends.

But I would never tell this to my mother.

She would use it as a chisel or a wedge and wouldn't stop hammering at me until I confessed that I believed in something. And I would, just to get her to leave me alone, when in fact I believe in nothing, and never have.

The Buddha's serene smile and Jesus' 70s-style beard are comforting cultural icons, but I do not have any illusions about anything beyond that. My Jesus action figure is a combination of painted polymers configured over a pair of wheels; my teakwood Buddha is a mass-produced emblem of serenity; my prayer beads give me something to hold onto when I need something to hold onto. There is nothing more—no miracles, no immanence, no transubstantiation or eternal permanence. For me, there doesn't need to be. But my mother refuses to accept this.

"You have to believe in something," she says.

And I shake my head and shrug.

Because of our religious differences, my mother and I haven't spoken in weeks—not since our argument about Darwin's "theories." This argument started when my mother took a blue marker to an article I'd read about evolution and highlighted every occurrence of the words "possibly," "maybe," "perhaps," "thinks," and "believes" in order to prove how shifty the ground was upon which this whole "monkey science" was based. After this demonstration, I was called to defend, all by myself, one hundred and fifty years of evolutionary biology.

"Explain consciousness," she said.

"It's an accident of—"

"Explain love."

"Sexual selec—"

"Explain why we have more ribs than your father."

"Oh Christ," I said.

"Exactly."

I became exasperated. "It's the twenty-first century we're living in here," I said. "How can you still think that way?"

She clammed up and gave me a look. I held my ground, even as the look grew darker and her lower jaw set, her chin pushed forward, and her lips pressed together, zippered shut.

"How?"

She exhaled a thin, pissed-off whistle. "If you knew where I was raised—how I was raised—how my mother and her mother before her were raised—maybe you would understand how I 'think that way'." She held up her fingers and made sarcastic quotation marks with them.

I rolled my eyes and threw up my hands. Before leaving, I said that word that all mothers hate to hear: "Whatever."

But she had a point.

Lorenza, Margarita, and my mother Madeleine were born and raised in the Republic of Panama, that narrow isthmus that connects two continents, as well as two oceans, two worlds, two lives: North America to the South, the New World to the Old, my mother's life to mine.

I have never been there.

My knowledge of Panama comes to me mediated through old photographs and post cards, bright molas and faded gourds. It seems to me a strange and exotic place, remote and unknown. I feel no connection to it, for although I am twenty-five percent Panamanian, in appearance I favor my father, who is a Swede.

My father and I are as white as marshmallows; we burn easily, and insects love us. We belong in Minnesota, with Swedes and Norwegians as deficient in melanin as we. We certainly don't belong to the jungle. But my mother, who is half Panamanian and half Norwegian—with her black hair, brown eyes, and smooth skin that never wrinkles, even though she is fifty-five—does. She lived the first twenty years of her life in and out of the Canal Zone, in Panama, collecting sea shells at low tide and sipping chilled coconut juice, right from the pipa, in her home in Cocolí.

I feel wistful, thinking things over, about how little I know of this period of my mother's life. And I feel ashamed. I cannot stand feeling ashamed and make up my mind to do something about this rift that has come between us and grown over the years. The idea comes to me on the edge of sleep, in the middle of the night, in a dream of hot green spaces. Why not? I know some Spanish. I have family down there. I have a credit card. Why not? I ask myself again.

So, after madly scrambling for cash and begging for an extension of my Citibank credit limit, I am traveling to Panama to see if I can figure out, after all these years, where my mother is coming from.

◦◦◦

MY AUNT BIBI picks me up at the Panama airport. Even though she has dyed her dark hair blonde, I recognize her immediately. Her resemblance to my mother is striking. They are sisters, after all, although the two of them haven't had a civilized conversation in years.

I was, in fact, amazed and touched when my mother showed me the e-mail she had written to her sister about my coming to Panama:

"You know how Lisa is. KEEP HER SAFE...Madeleine." I chose to ignore the first sentence and focus on the second.

"Wow," I said to my mom. "I can't believe you and Bibi are talking again."

"We're not talking," my mother said. "We're e-mailing. There's a difference."

"You're communicating," I insisted.

She "humphed" at me as I packed.

"Whatever happened with you two?" I asked. "You used to be so close."

She gives me a look from her arsenal of looks. "Don't lend her any money."

◦◦◦

BIBI TOWERS OVER the rest of the people in the waiting area of the airport, and her smile stretches ear to ear, bright red and Carmen Miranda wide. We hug, and all the Spanish I have been practicing comes

out in halting sentences, jumbled and twisting. It's not that I have to use
Spanish; like my mother, all my aunts and uncles are bilingual, but I
want to. I need to, because I am trying to learn to speak my mother's
language.

Bibi and I drag my duffel bag, which Bibi nicknames "el muerto" out
to her old red Tercel. Although she asks me to call her Elizabeth, which
is her real name, she is still Aunt Bibi to me. And I am her *tocaya*—her
namesake, since Elizabeth, which means "God Has Sworn" in Hebrew,
is my real name as well, and Lisa is just a diminutive of the way Elizabeth sounds in Spanish (A-lisa-bet).

Bibi's apartment in the banking district is lofty and sprawling, with
pale orange tile floors and lots of open space, including one big bedroom, one tiny bedroom that was the "maid's quarters" in earlier days,
a large laundry room, and a verandah. My Aunt Bibi is an iridologist
and herbalist, a modern day Panamanian curandera who heals with
herbs and eye charts, and her boyfriend Jose does massage therapy, so
there is also a therapy room and waiting area for their clients.

Once we drop off "el muerto" in the small side room that will be my
bedroom, Bibi and I sit down in her kitchen and drink hot tea. She
looks into my eyes and recommends a lengthy prescription of golden
seal, Dong Quai, and cascara sagrada. When I tell her that I have no
money with which to buy her herbs, she looks disappointed but doesn't
press. And, after an hour or so of bringing each other up to date, Bibi
looks at me firmly and says, "How's Mimi? How's my sister?"

I am unsure how to begin. "We fight all the time," I say. "I'm trying
to figure out where she's coming from."

"What do you fight about?"

I tell Bibi about the Darwin article.

"Well," she sips her tea. "I hope you don't believe in *that* nonsense."

"Wait a minute here." I switch back to English. "You don't believe in
evolution?"

"*De nada.*" Her hands fly out definitively. "I'm not related to any
monkey."

"But you're not a Christian?"

Bibi sits back in her chair and regards me as one might regard an
alien species who has crash-landed on her lawn in the pre-dawn light—

rubbing her eyes at this astonishing sight and asking herself, *Am I dreaming?*

"Of *course* I'm a Christian," she says.

"But you believe that herbs can heal and that my eyes reveal what's wrong with me?"

"Absolutely."

"But isn't that like witchcraft?"

Bibi looks at me sideways. "I have someone I want you to meet."

BIBI AND I get back into the car and drive to her friend Elisa's house, which is not a house, but a garage with a cement floor on a small side street. Elisa, a sixty year old woman without a wrinkle in her skin, opens the garage door and says *"Aunque mi casa es pobre estás bienvenida aquí."* (Although my house is poor, you are welcome here). *"Soy Elizabeth."*

We are now three generations of Elizabeths in one room. I wonder superstitiously if this carries any import and make a mental note to look this up in my book of superstition when I get back home.

Elisa is Cuban and makes a mean *ropa vieja,* a stewed and rope-like beef. After eating, we have an extended conversation about the powers of voodoo, which Elisa has (*gracias a Dios,* she says) left behind. She tells of an evil Babalao, a voodoo priest, who made cloth dolls, cement saint dolls, and who specialized in bloodletting goats and doves.

She speaks quickly, omitting the usual hard r's, so Bibi has to translate:

"I had a saint doll once, and it gave me nothing but trouble. I had one made in my image and it started to fall apart when I came here to Panama, so I rolled it up and made a little place for it inside my suitcase. But when I got here, do you know what happened? The rats ate it. They had a feast! And I threw that saint doll away because I realized then that there is only one true God and his son Jesus Christ."

Bibi nods solemnly after translating this statement and adds, "That sort of belief system is a form of slavery. It's so incredible that people believe in it today."

Elisa clears the table and brushes me aside, in mock outrage, when I try to help. I am the guest, she insists, and I will do nothing but eat. Once the table is cleared, Elisa dims the lights, and my aunt Bibi pulls out a golden pendulum on a heavy gold chain.

"What's that for?" I ask.

"*Cállate,*" Bibi murmurs. I shut up and watch.

Bibi whispers above the chain. All I can make out is "*Cuanto tiempo...cuanto tiempo.*" The rest is too fast to follow. The room grows cold, and the hairs on my forearm rise. The pendant sways, swings four times in a circle, then slows and hangs straight.

Bibi closes her eyes. "*Cuatro meses.*" Four months.

Elisa's eyes shine over. She grabs her apron in her fist and squeezes. Afterwards, we thank her for lunch and leave.

Back in the sunlight, I watch the goose bumps on my arm retreat. I grab Bibi by the elbow. "What the *hell* was *that?*"

Bibi shakes me off gently as we climb into her car and explains that she was asking how long Elisa and her husband would have to wait before they would be able to join the rest of their family in Florida.

"Asking who?" I say. "Who were you asking?"

Bibi shrugs and smiles. "God."

✦

THAT NIGHT BIBI AND I stop at a small convenience store, *Bodega mi Amiga,* and buy a pint of ceviche and a case of Imperial, Panamanian beer, and sit on her verandah, watching the storm clouds roll in. The ceviche is good—the beer is essential. I slug down a bottle without blinking and devote myself to spreading the ceviche on a cracker. Bibi sips slowly, content, and regards me fondly.

"What did you think of Elisa?"

I hiccup. "She seems nice."

We are quiet for a moment, before I ask: "You don't see a contradiction?"

"What do you mean?"

"Between your faith in God and witchcraft. Between Elisa's faith in God and witchcraft?"

She holds up her index finger. "There is only one true God."

I sigh and shake my head. I think about Elisa's brush with the Babalao and start laughing.

"You know," I say to Bibi. "I thought Babalao was the name of Ricky

27

Ricardo's club on *I Love Lucy*."

"That was *Babalu*." She laughs too, and throws a cracker at my head. "Go to bed."

⟶◉⟵

As I lie in bed I think of *tulivieja*, the ash eater.

When I was little my mother terrified me with stories of this old witch who lurked at the river's edge and stole children, carved them up with her long ragged claws, then burned them up and ate their ashes on the sandbank. These are the bedtime stories I grew up with—followed by a prim "say your prayers" before lights out. No wonder I needed a night light until I was sixteen.

Here, now, in Bibi's apartment in Panama, with the storm winds blowing the hanging laundry outside my bedroom so the shirtsleeves dance like the arms of ghosts, I turn the bathroom light on, even though I am twenty-seven years old, and tell myself that I don't believe in anything.

I sleep fitfully, dreaming of golden pendants, voodoo priests, and Ricky Ricardo yelling "Baba-lao!" in a roofless nightclub, as ash rains down on his stage.

⟶◉⟵

The next morning Bibi and I begin our drive north, through the provinces of Panama, Veraguas, Coclé, and Herrera, to Chiriquí, where my grandmother Margarita is from.

It will take us seven hours to get to Davíd, so we stop in Santiago and have a full meal of pork chops and *patacones*. Since I arrived in Panama yesterday, I have felt awkward, conspicuous, and out of place. Eating the *patacones*, however, is like coming home. My mother makes them for me every year on my birthday, if she can find green plantains to squash flat and fry, and it's nice to eat them and not have to explain to anyone what they are.

After lunch we drive through rainstorms in Bibi's old Tercel. As a lightning bolt strikes, illuminating her face, Bibi turns to me and says. "You really don't believe in God?"

I nod, holding onto the armrest of the Tercel as the lightning snakes down. "You really do?"

Bibi nods firmly. "Yes. I believe that I am on this earth for a *purpose*—that I was created by a loving God who has *plans* for me."

I snort. "You sound like Grandma." We both know this is not a compliment. My earliest memory of my grandmother involves her telling me about Armageddon in her house in Florida—before whacking me with her *chancleta* for eating too many cookies. *Chancleta*, which means slipper, was in fact the first word I learned in Spanish, because my grandmother was always whacking me—or threatening to whack me—with it.

"Do you know anything about your grandmother?" Bibi asks. "My mother."

I snort again. "She has a wicked forehand."

The rain drops smear on the windshield, giving the car a darkly luminous glow. Bibi sighs sadly, taps her hands on the steering wheel, and tells me about Margarita Gomez.

∞

MY GRANDMOTHER, MARGARITA GOMEZ, was born in a volcanic crater in the province of Chiriquí, Panama in 1922.

She and her mother Lorenza lived near the Chiriquí River, in the dense mountain jungle, and Margarita, whose name means Daisy, remembers being four years old. Lorenza sent her out to get water from the river, and as she bent over the water, she saw jaguar footprints in the mud at the river's edge. After that, she was afraid of being mauled every time she stepped outside.

She never knew her father, Juan Gomez. One day when she was still an infant he went out hunting and never came back, and she and Lorenza never knew for sure if he was dead or had just abandoned them.

As Margarita grew older, she and Lorenza looked more like nesting doll sisters than mother and daughter. They were both petite and well rounded, with skinny legs, flat feet, and big soft bosoms. They had the same black hair and intense black eyes; they shared the same clothes; and they lived in the same small house with its dirt floor, tin roof, and thin walls.

When Margarita was thirteen, Lorenza, desperate for money, sold

29

her into marriage to a man named Rafael.

He beat her. He raped her. And, after she had borne a son to him at the age of fourteen, she fled back with the baby to Lorenza in Volcán.

She stayed with Lorenza and found work as a maid and cook at the home of a wealthy lawyer in the nearby town of David. She worked there until she met the man who would, as they say in the breathless manner of soap operas and romance novels, change her life forever.

My grandfather came from North Dakota to Colombia in the thirties to work for the United Fruit Company. He was a civil engineer; he managed sewage lines and drain pipes and designed garbage sluices for a living. He was tall and lean and spoke schoolbook Spanish with a clean, neat accent. After some time he was transferred to Panama, which wasn't so much of a transfer as it was a change of name, since Panama was part of Colombia before the U.S. "liberated" it in 1905.

One day my grandfather saw Margarita, my grandmother, kneading bread outside on a hot day in the Chiriquí summer. His pulse quickened beneath the pressed lapels of his linen suit. He approached her and said in Spanish, "I would like to taste some of that bread."

They were married shortly afterwards. She was eighteen; he was thirty-five. It was his first marriage and her second. The Catholic Church refused to recognize their marriage, since she was still legally married to Rafael. Rafael took her son because the law and the Church favored the father in these cases. The Church never did recognize her marriage, and Margarita had nothing more to do with papists. She became a Jehova's Witness soon after.

I am beginning to understand why.

☙❦❧

BIBI AND I ARRIVE IN DAVID and stay at the hotel Puerta del Sol. The rooms are clean, with high, firm narrow beds, yellow bed covers, white walls, and cherry wood doors. After a light dinner in the hotel restaurant, we fall asleep early, listening to the rainfall against the window panes.

The next morning we drive around David and Volcán, looking at the coffee farms that line the green mountains. It rains, and the sky looks like a flat gray screen. The lightning bolts strike, the sky flashes, and the earth shakes the slate clean.

We drive to the Chiriquí River, and hike above the churning water. I wonder which part of this river's mud held the footprints of a jaguar that frightened my grandmother so, but I'll never know, because Bibi tells me that Lorenza's house is long gone.

As we leave the mountains I fight sleep. "Why did they leave?" I ask, yawning. "When did they move?"

"Daddy got a job working for the Canal Zone," Bibi says. "He was a civil servant. He and your Grandpa Swanstrom worked together in the same office."

I shake my head. "That must have been something."

"It was." Bibi laughs. "They didn't get along too well. We'll go to the Canal Zone tomorrow, if you like. I'll show you where they worked. Where your mom and dad went to high school. Where they fell in love."

I would like that. I tell her so before I fall asleep.

~☙~

THE CANAL ZONE is a ghost town. What was once Cocolí, Rodman, and Balboa High is now nothing more than a group of empty houses in extreme disrepair, sagging above cement blocks where neighborhoods once stood. Empty.

Yet in a way, the emptiness of the Zone makes it easier for me to imagine my parents being here in the sixties—my mom in her high heels and knee-length skirt, walking to the Kingdom Hall on Sundays; my dad playing football on the empty field behind Balboa High; my Grandpa Swanstrom saving his pennies until he could go back to Minnesota with my Grandma Anne; my Grandpa Berg cutting his own way through the saw grass with a machete to make a shortcut to his house on Nicobar Lane; my grandmother grinding corn and talking endlessly about The Lord.

And the Cocolí pool.

"Your parents' whole romance took place at that pool," Bibi says, and I can see why. Like all pools, it is bright, aqua-blue, clear and cool. But the heat here is something, hotter than Costa Rica, way hotter and more humid than Florida, where I was born, and I can see how that pool would have been like paradise during this kind of weather.

I imagine my dad sitting on the lifeguard chair, a stripe of zinc down his nose, my mom climbing out of the water; him seeing her, her seeing him.

An armed guard on a bicycle interrupts my thoughts. We aren't supposed to be in here, poking around. The whole area is under the jurisdiction of the ARI (*Autoridad de la Region Interoceanica*), which took charge of the redistribution of land after 2000.

The armed guard stops his bike, adjusts his gun. He speaks into his walkie talkie and looks at us suspiciously.

"There used to be a swing set, playgrounds, and a movie theatre when I was a girl," Bibi explains to the guard in Spanish.

He says, "There's nothing here now but mosquitoes."

Bibi remarks how the tables have turned—how it used be the Panamanians who couldn't come into the Zone, and now it's the other way around. The guard smiles and lets us go.

Bibi smiles back, turns to me and says, "Let's go see the canal."

⟳

IT SAYS IN THE MUSEUM that the Panama Canal is the "seventh wonder of the industrial world." It's not far-fetched. I now know why my dad was so eager to show me the locks at Sioux Saint Marie at the Canadian Border in Michigan's U.P when we lived there when I was nine. We saw a black bear cub cross the highway then, I remember, running out from a thicket of pine trees, a collision of nature and technology.

Here, now, is another such collision.

The canal is fifty miles long, a green-chambered river, surrounded by jungle. The lake locks don't even compare.

"A man, a plan, a canal—Panama," Bibi says. "It's a palindrome."

"That's my mom's favorite."

Mine is "Satan, oscillate my metallic sonatas," but I decide not to share that with Bibi.

I smile to myself, thinking of the time my mother confiscated my homemade Ouija Board, and burned it right in front of me, and I realize, taking in the canal—the wall of jungle surrounding it, the dizzy green smell of it, and the waters of two oceans flowing through it—that I have never understood my mother.

Or my grandmother.

I admit to a certain fascination with Lorenza, the witch, but that hardly counts as understanding.

But talking with my Aunt Bibi is helping me come to terms with it all.

We leave the locks when Bibi looks at her watch. "C'mon. We need to go before it closes."

"What?"

"The cemetery."

∾⟆∿

THE *JARDÍN DE PAZ* IS HUGE, sprawling, and unmarked except for a few clay stone disks not much larger than silver dollars.

Lorenza Nuñez, my great-grandmother, is buried here.

Many of the graves are unmarked except for even smaller clay stones that say only the grid coordinates of the burial point (G7, for example). But Lorenza has a real tombstone, right next to her recently deceased last husband (she had three), whom she hated and on whose account she had prayed to God that she might forget him, his name, his face, and everything about him, so when she saw him, even though they were neighbors, she would not recognize him.

"And you know what?" she said to Bibi. "One day I saw a man standing across the way and he looked familiar but I couldn't say who he was— and later on they told me it was Rudolfo Valdéz."

Even so, they buried him next to Lorenza, and I wonder, superstitiously, if she recognizes him now, lying in the earth beside her. But wondering this is ridiculous, since I don't believe in such things. Still, I shiver, even in the heat.

When Bibi finds out they've buried him next to her, she sucks in air and whistles. She says, "She wouldn't have liked that. *Hubiera protestado.*"

"This is the first time you've been to see her grave?" I ask.

"That's right."

"But she's been dead for five years!"

Bibi shakes her head and looks at me like I am retarded. "That's what you don't understand, Lisa."

"What?"

"That she's not dead—that she'll never be dead."

She's right. That's what I don't understand.

◦◦◦

IT'S MY LAST NIGHT IN PANAMA, and Bibi and I go downstairs to her neighbor Mirna's apartment for a little party. Mirna, a tiny woman with soft skin and graying hair, is a seamstress from Colombia. She sews for Sandra Sandoval, a famous Panamanian performer who sings with her brother Sammy.

After two hours, Bibi's boyfriend Jose shows up and starts dancing. He drags me off the couch and I try not to step on his feet. Bibi orders Mirna's son to get some rum and limes, and the next thing I know everyone is tipsy.

Bibi turns to them, points to me, and says in slurred Spanish, "This one doesn't believe in God."

There is a dramatic silence after they all suck in air, gasping in shock. Great. "*Es que necesito probanza.*" I say. Proof.

Before I can qualify this statement any further, which might not even be possible, since I am half gone on *mojitos*, everyone in the room is offering up experiential evidence to support the existence of God and telling stories about supernatural occurrences in their respective Latin American countries.

Jose describes a Cuban method by which butterflies are used to talk to the dead.

Mirna reports seeing a dead man who comes back to life in Colombia.

Bibi spins the familiar Panamanian *tulivieja* story.

Yolanda, a lady from the Dominican Republic, describes the lights that come out of the tombs of cemeteries at night but concedes that this happens everywhere.

And Eva, who hasn't said a word all evening, explains all there is to know about witches.

An interesting fact about witches is that they can take the form of pigs, turkeys, horses, snakes and monkeys but not cats, dogs, or turtles. Eva advises me that if the witch is a monkey it is best to use salt, which will burn it.

"Yes, yes," Mirna interrupts. "But if you are walking down the street and see a pig on the corner who keeps giving you dirty looks, you may be seeing a witch in disguise."

Eva continues. "And if every day the same pig gives you the same evil look, then you may be sure of it. Once you are sure, you must scoop a handful of grain (be it rice or wheat or corn) and approach the disguised witch and throw the grain at the pig's feet.

"Then you must say: 'I know that you are a witch, and I want you to pick up these grains, one by one'."

At this point the witch should turn back into a witch, but she will be naked. And due to her need for order, she will be compelled to pick up each grain, one by one, because she will not be able to bear to see them scattered and disordered in the street.

I am not sure what happens after she finishes picking up the grain, but I imagine by then I would be long gone.

"But what if you aren't sure if the pig is a witch?" I ask. "What if the witch keeps her identity a secret?"

"I'll tell you!"

Eva's *ex-suegra* was a witch who put a curse on Eva after she broke up with her son.

"How did you know she cursed you?" I ask.

"I came home from work," she says, "and before I even walked in the door, my brother ran half-naked from the house, terrified. When I asked him why he was so afraid he pointed inside, to our dining room table."

There, all of their pets (several cats and dogs) were standing with their hackles raised and their ears back. They surrounded the table, all staring at one fixed spot. The dogs were growling and the cats were hissing, but not at each other—at the spot.

"And you know what was there?" She asks, raising her eyebrows at me.

"What?" I ask.

"*Absolutely nothing.*"

So Eva consulted her priest, who confirmed her suspicions that her *ex-seugra* was the cause of all this mischief.

The priest advised Eva to put out three glasses on the dining room table and fill the first one halfway with water, the second halfway with salt, and the third halfway with coffee.

"Your *priest* told you to do this?" I ask.

"*Claro.*" She says, as if to say "Who else?" She was to leave them out at night, and if the next morning the salt was mixed up with the coffee, it would mean that the witch had been personally at Eva's house, working mischief in the flesh. However, if the salt and coffee were mixed up with the water, it would mean that the witch had cast her spell remotely. Fortunately for Eva, none of the contents shifted throughout the course of several nights—of this Eva is certain because she looked at each glass with a magnifying glass.

"Did you have any more problems?" I ask.

"No." She shakes her head and sips on her *mojito*, daintily picking a mint leaf from between her teeth. "*Gracias a Dios, no.*"

My mother is starting to make sense.

⚬

THE NEXT MORNING, Bibi and I have a tearful farewell, promising each other we'll write more often in the future. I hope we do.

"*Que Dios te bendiga,*" she says in parting, and I feel blessed.

As I fly back home to California, on TACA airlines, hungover and tired, I find myself wondering about the in-between-ness of it all. Christian, witch, priest, and witness, you are first one thing, then another. Then you are neither, and then, finally, you are all. You are backwards and forwards, frontward and back, trying to make sense of it all.

I think fondly of the gold Buddha on my mantle and hope he's not getting too dusty in my absence. I promise myself to give him a good polish when I return, not because I think I will be re-born, saved, or resurrected by the Buddha's power, but because I need, as we all need, to believe in something outside of ourselves, something greater, something good. I don't believe in God, but I believe in flesh and blood, skin and bone, and our uncanny ability to be two contradictory things at the same time.

Standing in front of the glossy locks of the Panama canal, Bibi said, "It's a palindrome." It strikes me that I have visited Panama in 2002, the year of the palindrome, and that although this year will pass, I am in it now, straddling two worlds, a fleshly bridge, a divided yet connected being. Panama connects more than oceans, more than continents, more than cultures, waters, and lives. It also moves between and mixes different poles, peoples, religions, and times.

Staring out the window of the airplane at the clouds and oceans below me, I think that each of us is a palindrome made of muscle, made of blood, that reaches back to the past, even as we throw out grappling hooks towards the future. Lorenza, Margarita, my mother, and I—we all started out inside the bellies of bodies of different times, different places, and are products of the "then" as much as of the now.

When I see my mother, perhaps I will tell her this. I will say, "I do not understand you; perhaps I never will. But I know that you are part of me as surely as we breathe, as surely as we dream." I will take her hands in mine and examine her small palms.

"I am not a witch," I will say. "And I do not believe what you believe. But I recognize your flesh in my hands, your blood in my veins, and the black witch's mole on the back of your neck, which is also on mine, and I love you; and know you love me. I am your daughter, and you are your mother's daughter, and one day perhaps I will have a daughter, and I will point her backwards, even as she moves forward in time, and she will see that she is her mother's daughter, farther and farther back down the line, until it's harder and harder to see us, to see you, to see me, all the way back to Eve." ◆

Jo Ann Pantanizopoulos

GETTING RELIGION

Several times in my life I have tried to avoid getting wet in the name of Jesus. Walking down that aisle to the preacher who would make me kneel and talk about serious stuff was just too much to bear. I preferred staying in my seat and pretending to be baptized. Each year an evangelist visited our First Baptist Church in Roswell, New Mexico, and each year I continued to pretend. When I was in fourth grade in 1957, I had an especially ardent Sunday school teacher. As we assembled in our rows waiting for the evangelist to finish his tirade and call forth those who wanted to allow Jesus Christ to be their everlasting savior, I was worried my teacher would find me out. Standing behind me, she leaned over and whispered in my ear, "Jo Ann, are you ready to take Jesus Christ into your heart? Are you ready, honey? Don't you think it's time you took the first step to the River Jordan?" Like a pesky gnat, she leaned over again and again whispering those words, "Are you ready, Jo Ann? Honey, are you ready?" Wishing the evangelist would wind up his call, I shook my head and told her, "No, I just don't think I'm ready yet." I couldn't wait to get out of there. I felt pinned in by the teacher behind me, the red-faced evangelist calling for heathens like me to walk towards him, and the long expanse of red carpet I was not ready to tread.

And so I continued to pretend whenever I visited a church. Then I met and fell in love with a Greek god named Yanni in 1967, and my journey began. Three years later, we decided to marry in his hometown, Thessaloniki, Greece.

WE BEGAN THE PAPERWORK which would allow pagan little twenty-
two year-old me to marry Greek Orthodox thirty year-old him. A passport, birth certificate, and baptism papers were all we needed to send
over to the Greek authorities. Uh, baptism papers—don't have any. "No
problem, *glika mou* my sweetheart, you can get baptized in the Greek Orthodox church; in fact, you *have* to if we are to get married," my Greek
god told me. Only baptized Christians could marry in the church. I
wasn't totally unopposed to becoming Greek Orthodox. Prior to my
decision to marry Yanni, I had attended several friends' weddings in
Greek churches and the big receptions that always followed. The Greeks
seemed to enjoy themselves dancing, drinking and smoking, while still
maintaining their spirituality in beautiful rituals complete with candles
and incense. I could deal with that.

Father Apostolos arranged for us to have the baptism on August 1 at
a nearby church named *Ahyropéytos*, which means "made of bricks rein-
forced with straw," at 7:00 am. Although it would be held in a side
chapel that had a copper baptismal font set into the 5th century stone
floor, he believed it best to meet early and in the side chapel for two
reasons: It would be cooler and people who stop by the church to pray
and light a candle on their way to work wouldn't peek in at me—the
unique phenomenon of the young American girl getting baptized, the
xeni, the foreign one. Children born in Greek Orthodox families are always baptized as infants, so adult baptisms were truly the odd occasion.
Just my husband's parents, his three sisters with their families together
with my mother and brother planned to be there.

For about a week before this event, Father Apostolos said I needed
kateéheisis or catechism, instruction in Orthodoxy, but because time was
short, he said we could do some intensive lessons. Each afternoon
Yanni and I went to Father Apostolos' apartment for two hours. Together with his wife *presvytéra* and two deeply religious spinsters, Despina
and Apollonia, sitting in his study, Father explained my new religion in
Greek while Yanni translated into English. Priests' wives aren't addressed by their actual names; they're addressed with just *presvytéra*,
which means wife of a priest, or officially, *presvytéros*. With wide-eyed

wonder, as if they were hearing his words for the first time, Despina and Apollonia took notes and nodded their heads in agreement. Both ladies were middle-aged and had never married. Despina was rather short while Apollonia was tall by Greek standards. Neither wore make-up, and both wore dark blue or brown dresses with long-sleeves. They adored Father Apostolos and his wife and seemed to follow them everywhere. Unlike many priests I had seen up until then, Father Apostolos always smiled and seemed genuinely happy. Each afternoon, Father plodded on, trying to summarize almost 2,000 years of Greek Orthodoxy, and soon my eyes grew heavy even though *presvytéra* always served us sweet thick coffee in tiny cups and a spoon of *vanilia*, a thick white vanilla-tasting soft candy, in a glass of cold water before we started. To stay alert, I asked Yanni, "I'm falling asleep. Are we going to the seaside taverna tonight with Dimitra and Thanos? What's the name of that fried cheese we had the other night?" And Yanni translated back to Father, "My fiancé asked if you could please expand on the importance of the seven sacraments." My "Yanni, how much longer? I love your eyes" translated into "Father, she wants to know if there is more than one path to heaven."

Father Apostolos was so taken with my enthusiasm for Orthodoxy, my baptism, and our marriage that he asked if I would do a huge favor for him: Read the book of Matthew in English and have Despina and Apollonia record it on a tape recorder. One evening the two spinsters arrived at my mother-in-law's home carrying their tape recorder and presenting Yanni and me with a gift from Father Apostolos, a King James version of the Bible—in English. As I read Matthew into that tape recorder, Despina and Apollonia ran back and forth bringing me glasses of water. I finished in about three hours.

In preparation for my baptism, my mother-in-law chose Kyria Euphrosyne as my godmother, my *nouná*. Since Kyria Euphrosyne's son had been Yanni's friend in the United States, she and my mother-in-law became friends as well. A tiny bird of a woman and devoted to the church, my *nouná* dressed plainly like Despina and Apollonia. Since it's customary for a newly baptized baby to dress in all new white clothing, she bought me a new white bra, white underpants, white sandals, and a white dress. She also made me a white cotton gown and embroidered a small red cross at the neck. And for privacy, Father Apostolos asked Despina and Apollonia to hang up a cloth curtain in a corner of the chapel where I could change my clothing.

In addition to Despina and Apollonia, Father had assembled several of his and *presvytéra's* female friends to serve as the choir. As they began singing a Byzantine chant, I entered wearing my white cotton robe, naked underneath. The service was interrupted several times when Father Apostolos paused and let my *nouná* spit on the devil three times: *ftou, ftou, ftou.* God, I hope he doesn't make me say that, I thought to myself. Then Yanni whispered, "Jo, spit on the devil three times just like your *nouná* did."

"Flou, flou, flou," I floundered almost extinguishing the candle I held with my spit. I should have practiced, I thought. At one point, my *nouná* led me over behind the curtain and lifted up my gown. While she motioned for me to hold it up over my head, she grabbed a squirt bottle of "blessed" olive oil and started to rub it over my head and body. "*Yirna!*" she said and motioned for me to turn around and let her do my backside and the bottom of my feet. I was mortified, and she giggled. With the gown down once again covering me, we stepped out of the curtain and I slipped my way back towards the font. I envisioned this episode as a short story entitled "Fear and Humiliation: The Early Years."

All the while, strangers kept peeking in the door and soon the small chapel was packed with people I'd never seen before. The body heat and candles in the room made that August morning even warmer. After a few more "ftou's" and "flou's," Father filled a large brass pitcher with warm water and motioned for me to step forward into the font. As he poured the water over me, he said "*En Iordani vaptisomeni sou. Kyrie elaison. Kyrie elaison. Kyrie elaison.*" I had reached the River Jordan, and my baptismal name was *Iosifina*. I felt the white cotton robe attach itself to my oily body. Trying to concentrate on what the priest was saying and where he was pouring, I felt like I was at a wet t-shirt contest in my white gown. When I tried to remove the plastic-like cloth hugging my chest, it became glued to my bottom. "*Apataxou ton Satana?* Do you reject Satan?"

"*Apatasome.* I reject him," replied my *nouná*.

At last my *nouná* handed me a white towel that I used to wipe my face and hold discreetly over my chest. I followed her back to the curtain. Each step stretched my wet, oily gown over my skin, preventing me from running for cover. Behind the curtain, *nouná* began to remove my gown and handed me my new bra, panties, and white sleeveless dress. Modest and plain, the dress was made of white polyester, and the seamstress had added some gathers below the neckline. Sliding awkwardly in my new white sandals, we exited the curtain. Friends, strangers, and gawkers came to me, kissed me on both cheeks and shook my hand. *"Na zisete!* May you live a long life!" And to my *nouna,* *"Panda axia!* Always able!"

Although it was only 8:30 am, the room was suffocating and hot, my jaws hurt from smiling and I felt like crying from all the people and *"Na zisete's"* swirling around me. But soon we left the church and walked the two blocks back to the apartment. Friends and family gathered there for a big meal of *moussaka, pastitsio, taramosalata, fasolakia, horiatiki salata, galaktoboureko,* and more. The dress was sticking to my sweaty, oily body—even my glasses were sliding down my nose. I could barely see through them from all the times I had to nudge them up with my oily hand. Miserable, I asked Yanni if I could take a quick bath and then rejoin the guests. After what seemed like a lengthy discussion with his mother, he came back to me and asked if I couldn't wait three days to take my bath. He explained the custom is to wait for three days to wash the baby and the baby's clothes after infant baptisms, and I should do the same.

So many Greek customs are linked to the number three—the Father, the Son, and the Holy Spirit. A bride and groom walk around the altar table three times, take three sips of wine after their *koumbaros* exchanges their crowns three times. "Ftou. Ftou. Ftou"—three times. Blessings are said three times. People make the sign of the cross three times. When I told him I just *had* to take a bath and couldn't wait three days, he said that they would have to turn on the heat in order to make hot water for my bath. Not only did I feel like a big nuisance but a *miserable* big nuisance. I glided with oily feet into the bathroom, sat down on the toilet, held my greasy face in my oily hands and waited for Yanni's word that the water was ready for my bath. Soon, my mother-in-law and Yanni came into the bathroom to explain to me not to let the water go down the drain after I finished. Because holy water cannot enter the sewer, it must be poured either in the sea or on living plants.

Intent on relieving my uncomfortable state, I discarded the thought about what would happen to the water after I bathed. After they left, I took a wonderful bath even though it took several soapings and shampooings to remove all the oil. Feeling clean and refreshed, I left behind me a bath tub full of holy water complete with gray, oily soap scum. My appetite returned, my smile reappeared, and I enjoyed the party.

After everyone left, I began to help my future sisters-in-law with the dishes. As I was drying the last of the pots and pans, I saw my mother-in-law walk down the hallway and enter the bathroom. With a dish towel in my hand, I followed her. She leaned over and began scooping up the murky bathwater into some buckets. Embarrassed that I had made extra work for her, I told her *"Signome, mamá!* I'm sorry, mamá!" She laughed and began singing from a popular song on the radio, *"Signome, pou se agapisa poli!* I'm sorry I loved you so much!" Mamá carried my bath water all the way back to the garden of *Ahyropéytos,* a blue bucket in each hand. It took two trips. ◆

GANDHI'S WINDOW
by Mark DeKay

Mark DeKay

Teachings from Bapu Kuti

*I*t was a tough choice between inhaling sub-continental dust with the windows down and sharing the exotic odors, windows up, of the five people touching all sides of me. The share-taxi, really a Land Cruiser-sized Jeep, from Ellora to Aurangabad was fifteen rupees each, about thirty cents. What a deal, I thought, until one by one, the shared seating was filled to the overflowing occupancy of 24. The Jeep blared Hindi music, and no modesty remained among the passengers. Thirty kilometers later, I bought a ticket for the luxury bus to Jalgaon which included a free Hindi movie and one cushioned seat per person. At the hotel, hot water arrived in buckets. The next morning's train arrived at Wardha by 11am, where I caught a yellow auto-rickshaw, the last in a medley of a half-dozen transportation modes on my trek to *Sevagram*, Gandhi's last ashram.

Twelve to fifteen permanent residents still live at Sevagram, plus numerous visitors, long and short term. They practice simple agricultural lives and ascetic principles. 2 pm: On tiny portable spinning wheels, thread from cotton the community grows is spun for at least twenty minutes, the time required to spin thread for one year's cloth. 5 pm: A simple, locally grown, delicious vegetarian meal is eaten while sitting on the floor, mostly in silence. Fresh, warm milk is served with *jaggerie,* a raw cane sugar. Yellow rice, mild *dal* (lentil stew), and all the *chapatis* you can eat complete the meal. 6 pm: During prayer, men and women are separated, as at dinner, and seated on the gravel courtyard, chanting while accompanied by a single one-string instrument. They meditate,

45

the sound of collective silence.

The quiet peace and simplicity of the place are profound. Their work, digging in the fields, spinning, cooking dinner, is their meditation. Their values are kindness and truthfulness. The buildings are simple mud huts with dung or stone floors and hand-made, clay-tiled roofs, all from local materials constructed by local village craftspeople—made by hands of humans, not the shaping of machines. I wondered about how such a simple way of building became an expression of *ahimsa,* non-violence. At its base, it is a kind of radical democracy, where one's desires do not expand with one's means, where what is taken from the earth is close to what one truly needs, and where fulfillment does not consume the resources required by another. It is also a place of humility, a physical expression of the spiritual equanimity among persons, of non-hierarchical relationships in a culture of caste, class, and bureaucracy.

Sevagram reminds me of what Gregory Bateson said about the basic unit of survival not being the organism, but rather, *organism-in-environment.* So close are we and it that we can not take a single breath, drink a cup of water, sleep one night under a roof, or eat a single bite of food that was not purified and provided by nature's ecological processes. At *Sevagram,* this is easy to see, but it is much harder at home, where natural process is covert. Perhaps we cannot say that nature is something to be connected with or to. We cannot talk meaningfully about reducing human impacts on an external nature. You and I and they and our environment are one living system. The connection with or dissociation from nature is in our perception. Does our connection to nature consist of removing our perceptual blocks?

Gandhi's house, *Bapu Kuti,* as the residents call it, is a small house with a small entry porch, a sitting room with woven floor mats for a few people, a small work space for Gandhi, a guest room, a place to care for the sick, an open verandah, and a not-so-Indian-style bathroom with a custom-built sit-down toilet — altogether perhaps 450 square feet. Such a small place contains such large lessons, even for me today. I left architectural practice because I was weary of working on houses in which neither I nor anyone in my family could ever afford to live. I took up research and teaching to influence more people and more buildings to evolve toward ecological integrity. This small home, the joy of the people here, and the modest life of the millions I have seen on the journey to *Bapu Kuti* force me to reconsider what I am doing and whether I am asking the right questions.

In a place so raw, so far down on the consumer food chain, it is clear that human community, even the city itself, is existentially, fundamentally dependent on nature, a nature which is "right here," *inside*, as much as it is ever "out there." If we destroy the physical landscape, then life will die. However, if we destroy all biological things, the material landscape will survive. Life will return to dust. Similarly, without the living landscape, there can be no cultural city. The mind is alive, but all that is alive is not mind. Biological life survives without human culture, but not vice versa.

Bapu Kuti makes one keenly aware of how little one actually needs to live a dignified life. This, in turn, leads to another, more powerful question. Is it not perverse to see industrialized technology as the progressive development for human habitat? Is my softer, eco-path version of technology much better? I suspect that I, and the whole organic-tech green movement, am off-course by several orders of magnitude. Certainly mere resource efficiency and human comfort are not measures worthy of constructing a new model of building. The spareness of Gandhi's home amplifies simple rituals, the circular events of community and companionship. These people live well. They have friends, books, intellectual lives, enough to eat, and human connections and care of the kind rarely seen. But they have no real material wealth.

Back home, there exists the *natural* environment and the *built* environment, and these incredibly separate things set up all kinds of thorny dualisms. We think ourselves into conceptual corners with these modern differentiations, often rising to pathological dissociations of self, culture, and nature. Yet here, the land is *alive*; it is a complex of forces which flows from bedrock to buildings to birds above. These are the forces that keep life going, the ecological services that conservation biologists tout but city dwellers never experience. I can also *see* the land at *Bapu Kuti* as a place that nurtures minds and souls, where nature restores us, where our relationship with the environment is participatory, where we develop *in* the environment. People here have shifted their perception; they know the land as an extension of their lives. How might we not only see the land as the place we *inhabit*, but also as a place that helps to define who we are, a place from which we cannot be separated?

The lesson of Gandhi's house is also about the non-essentialness of convenience, about the non-separateness of living and working, and ultimately, of self and other. From my modernist training in design school, I imbibed the view that embellishment evidences quality in buildings. I still carry the embedded cultural story that comfort equals luxury and that quality of life improves with size. Yet, here I see virtue and beauty in a humane minimalism, the kind of inconvenience that filters out the irrelevant and allows the perennial qualities in us to surface. It is evident here that there is a different phylum of time. Though there are clocks and watches, there are also bells and chimes, sunrise and sunset, summer and winter, field work and returning from the field, cooking and being cooked for, caring and being cared for, exposure to the elements and protection from them.

The contrast is immense between my home—with its isolation from the rhythms of place—and the pervasive connections to sky, sun, shade, and breeze found here. Here, a machine does not conquer the midday heat, so there is rest and time for reflection. Here, there is not the uniform space of home, where every square foot has light, heat, and cool whenever we desire. Fine work moves toward light. Spaces shift from sleep to work to social activity, while the activities migrate to follow shade or breeze from deep retreats to perimeter exposure and back. No single uses occur in specific places, our concrete placement in the rational matrix. Though there is electricity, it does not make bright the night. In the darkness there is time for talking with other souls and for mysteries of deep skies. There is time for rest—and quiet.

This non-separateness, an integral non-duality with nature, was made clear to me when I saw a communal water pump in the garden between a loose cluster of buildings. From the hand pump, a simple and elegant overflow channel guided spillwater along the ground to a trench, encircling mulch at the base of a single shade tree. Every time the pump was used, the tree was watered. The visibility of the linkage brought the lesson of the relationship to mind. In the heat of the day, the tree returned the favor as it cooled the ground for an afternoon of napping, reading, or contemplation. I imagined a city like this, where every form arose as a manifestation of our relationships to processes that we co-create with nature.

It's hard to describe what a place like this does to a person. It must be felt; it's like being immersed in a vibrant world where wholeness and integration, the profound sense of aliveness, are so palpable that one can no longer go on in the normal sleep-walking state. No one can say this of contemporary American neighborhoods, which are neither beautiful, nor do they feed our souls. Neighborhoods today are not great communities with shared civic lives. Neighborhoods today are not in sync with ecological processes. Anyone who looks carefully sees this is true. In each of these ways, the life in neighborhoods is diminished and each of us is also diminished. Each of us has to struggle harder to live, to find joy, to freely express our inner selves. We are more fragmented, more disconnected from our selves, from our society, and from our environment.

Healing the pathology of this dis—integration is a design problem. This dissociation of individuals from social groups, of rational engineering from its ecological context, of self-development from civic purpose, of micro-systems from their macro-containers—this is, in part, a design problem about the order of our cities. *The challenge of twenty-first century neighborhood design is the challenge of integration.* An integral neighborhood would reconnect art, culture and nature, the self, the social system, and the physical environment, weaving the usually independent approaches of aesthetic formalism, social engagement, and environmentalism.

On the second class train car heading south, small, hand-pinched terracotta cups and used banana leaf plates sail a meters-short flight from barred window to field on their return to become, in a year or so, flowers once again. *Sevagram* and its microcosm *Bapu Kuti* weave an indescribable simple/complex, organic, living network of person-community-place. "Chai. Coffee. Nescafe ," a barefoot boy chants. When was the last time I heard spoken in my civilized progressive design school the words, *beauty, truth, joy, freedom, love, non-violence,* or *social service?* When have I ever heard students called to virtue without apology? When have simplicity and surfing with nature's I/Thou flows been valued over complexity and expressionism? When have I asked my students to create places as environments for human and ecological development?◆

49

Camila Almeida

Immigration

A new home
was the reason
my aunts were left
alone crying
on the runway.

White clouds
peaks of angry mountains
begged us to stay,
unable to keep the
metal beast from
its destination.

We're landing on clouds,
I yell
fear clutches my heart
the sky could
drop us
and we could die.

It's snow, nieve
Mami whispers in that
gloom, doom, despair
voice we've grown
accustomed to.
The sound of wheels

IMMIGRATION

hitting ground
frightens my sister

she cries,
Quiero Abu!
I want grandma!

Callate, no digas nada
Don't embarrass mama
let her look like an
actress when she sees
Daddy, gone for months now,
smiles, open arms

Welcoming
his new immigrants
to a country
frozen in
winter

Where's the sun?
My brother asks
¿Dónde está el sol?

It's in Argentina,
Mami says...
El sol está en Argentina.

MAYPOLE SANCTUARY

*F*or my dissertation (and love, true), I climbed among the coastal cliffs and sea crags of Cres, Croatia, from Orlec to Belej, questing for them.

"Guide," he said to call him.

Guide was angry, contemptuous, his grudging monosyllables dropping like clotted cream, falling where they might.

"You're young to be so bleak." I could not resist small digs. He was of an age with me. I thought his interest caught. He was the angriest young man I had ever met. The stereotype would be lost on him. As it had been on me. Not because I'm a *she* and a rad about EC: Environmental Causes. I was as angry as you can—within reason—get about such matters. I still hadn't looked up what my father was always harping on with his "angry young men." I still hadn't looked up my father since that last Tail Flamer. Even if he was only an *English* professor, he should have known better.

Better not to let Guide think I was sighing over him.

I knew what I knew, though I didn't deign to tell Guide. That fewer than one hundred fifty remain. That if unsuccessful here, I'd move on to try to sight one of eight thought to be in the gorges of Paklenica National Park. Ugly, yes. By human standards, all vulturine is ugly. Bird of prey, yes, upon *dead* ovine. Guide wouldn't agree. I knew that much.

Guide went suddenly voluble: "What Miss think? You see them feed?"

I turned my ankle in response and fled, falling for eons. I heard the snaps, crackles, pops—smiled (Ok, Ok, *grimaced*) to think that here was another allusion Guide wouldn't get.

When the fall had had its way with me, I heard Guide call, Guide's echoes. Heard Silence—but for the pain that broadcast in Las Vegas neon, shock between the flashes. Broken leg, broken arm. That much I knew when I next knew anything.

I tried calling until my voice went. They'd find my backpack, surely. I'd lost it in the tumbling-barrel I'd been in. Rock polisher? What was that thing called? My brother had used one for a Boy Scout project one time.

In the sun's lowering I didn't want to see, he came. Still, I was grateful for the sudden shadow's cool. Until I thought what it must be, tried not to let my mind recite what I knew. They worked in teams before teams were fashionable. Even the environmentalists were taking up "team training," for God's sake! As if we wanted to appear sweetly reasonable. Jesus Christ!

The colony flies in comb formation. When one spots Prey—the word flamed cataract across the retina of my mind's eye—it circles to signal as this one was circling to signal now. Majestic, yes. Huge, yes. Long neck. I tried not to picture the neck's near-nudeness, rough skin, beak rapacious. Rapacious for me. Rapacious raptor. Rapt raptor. Don't unwrap! That last was for me.

Did the griffon vulture gather with its others—family *Accipitridae/ Cathartidae*—in anticipation of a death? That was the question, the mission that was mine. Did griffon vultures just fly straight in upon the instant prey was sighted?

I shivered, lugged my tub of guts—Dear Ole Dad ought to like that one at least—what was it? Hamlet mean to Polonius? Not to worry overmuch, but I needed more than an arras to hie me to about now. I was taking poetic license with *hie*. As best I could, I dragged myself along to reach a boulder bigger than my body. Hugged that hard-hearted rock for dear life. Cliché brought to serve another: Nature red in tooth and claw. I smile-grimaced again.

I tried to keep quiet but emitted inadvertent strains of agony through the bagpipes I now was. Maybe they'd convince the bird I wasn't dead enough to waste its time on. That word—*waste*—don't go there!

I began to pile taluses and scree. For weaponry? For a grave marker?

I couldn't have given the reason for the life of me. Which it probably was.

I'd just as soon not have remembered the day the lion died. He was far afield. Like me here. It was Guatemala's Chapín Park. He'd been put out to pasture so his keepers could line their coffers. My father finally at the breaking point. "Just shut up and enjoy goddamned Nature! Everything has to be a cause with you!"

This lion hadn't been prey to hunter, fire, famine, flood...he'd succumbed to loneliness, probably. For his lionesses and cubs pinioned elsewhere, doubtless, in another man-made veldt.

A vestige of his mightiness still stirred, though. He blocked our bus's way, sprawled across its path. The bus waited, giving majesty its due. No, giving us tourists our due. When at length the pictures had been taken, the driver raised a raucous din. That once-great creature, disdaining to look our way, slowly stood and shook himself. And then I saw the damaged forepaw. He bent it, tested earth gently, gingerly before he'd let foot take it. I wished the ailment merely thorn that I could play the saint to. My father was the first to tell me that one. Why didn't fathers remember?

The lion padded slowly, favoring that foot, until he was just off the road, then lay back down, head between front feet.

I saw them then. In every tree around, the vultures waited, watching, too, only quietly. Quite still. They knew a lion would die that day. That they and only they would perform his obsequies.

The cut bamboo the keepers had used to hide the fences' stolid iron was sending shoots forth in some few places. The lion would not renew. When I looked back, the vultures had mounded upon him. Made him a grave.

I saw a lion die that day. It was not *El Dia de los Muertos,* no "Day of the Dead." Nor had I *mano de león* (lion's paw) flowers to decorate *ofrenda,* offerings, for him. A lion died that day. Only the vultures gave him his ceremonial due.

Where was Guide? Would that Angry Young Man tell of my disappearing into a cataract? Let me go at that? At least disappearing into a cataract sounded romantic. Byron? Shelley? My father had always said I had a flair for dramatics.

Time. TIME. Make it pass. But productively. Until help could get to me.

I thought of my Old World uncle shaking his head wearily, sigh-saying,

"You cannot, Little Caterina, can never jump your shadow." He did not reference the one here now, the bird that shadowed me. Who was studying whom?

I dozed to fly on a lion-bodied griffin, reached to pat its eagle head. As it turned toward me to rictus-smile, the air hailed "hi-yi's." A heavy something plummeted glancingly, stilling ten feet away, trailing kite-tailed red ribbons.

My line of griffon vultures segued restively from it to me, wings a-stretch in place upon their chosen perches, answering my quest.

One roared upwards (so it seemed), went to check rich new plunder. His colleagues waited, lifting first one talon, then the other, great steer's-skull eyes probing me where I weakly rustled in my crumbling keep. I could have mewed like a lost kitten. Was I? Was I mewing like a lost kitten?

A call, high-pitched, raucous.

My watchers, as one, lifted, downed, mounded on the carrion creature, my scapegoat. I laughed—tried to—at the word's insulting irony. "*Scapegoat*. Watch and think. You must do something! You'd not end common carrion, would you? Think!"

But I was too fascinated to more than watch textbook fare served up as near-live-flesh. Sheep's entrails danced like ribbons round maypoles of griffon vultures. They follow herds of sheep. Sheepherders like them. They eat the dead, prevent disease, stop infection's spread.

Are they being used now in Europe's Foot-and-Mouth Crisis?

Will they wait to come for me dead?

The sobs—whose?

Shouldn't I keep quiet lest I distract them from the sheep? No! Let them know you're still alive!

Then the maypole walked, was standing over me. I escaped into oblivion.

Guide had reached me first. He'd sacrificed the foremost sheep he'd run upon, bell-wether of his father's flock, facts I did not know until much later.

His anger? He assumed I was another vulturous tourist type. Griffon vultures self-endanger. One fledgling a year at five years to maturity. Colonies travel widely, though the young can't fly more than 500 meters per day without wind's aid. Tourists—and local youths, Guide admitted—scare them into flight. They exhaust themselves, drop into the sea and drown. For people's amusement, cameras.

Guide and I were married. We're reestablishing griffon vultures—and sheep—on Krk Island, Croatia. We call our place "The Maypole Sanctuary." I gave Guide (still my pet name for him) the classiest bellwether you've ever seen as a wedding present. Our whole family, including Father, came for the wedding. He pronounced us poetic justice. ◆

WAIKIKI, JANUARY 2004
by Jo Angela Edwins

MANILA SIRENS

*O*ctober 1, 1975. Scarcely a month into the eighth grade, I got sent home for a fight. Not just me. Our whole school, even the teachers. This was no ordinary fight. This was a battle that rocked the city, a landmark in the nation's history. It was the "Thrilla in Manila: The Ali-Frazier Fight of a Lifetime."

As the only American in my class, I felt obliged to express interest in my dueling countrymen, but the truth was I knew less about them, about boxing in general, than anyone else, including my little brother, Travis, a sixth grader. I put fifty centavos, two days' ice-cream money, on Joe Frazier.

For two days, I went home hungry, while Travis grew fat off his winnings.

But then it seems I was hungry for most of that year we spent in the Philippines. In 1975 my father, a Baptist preacher, left his church in North Carolina to run a health clinic in a Manila slum. Travis and I thought he was the best dad in the world before he did that.

He'd made the decision when he learned that Mr. Foushee, the missionary he'd sent, got himself killed trying to cross a flooded street. Mr. Foushee didn't know about the open manhole under the waters until he stepped into it. "He resurfaced in Manila Bay," my father explained, "sixteen blocks from where he went under."

I told my mother that I liked it better when all Dad's work-talk was about God. She said I was being disrespectful to Mr. Foushee. She didn't know how Travis and I joked about his name, that it sounded like the

58

water as it sucked him under the street. *"Foo-sheee!"* we'd say with a great swishing sound like the flush of a toilet, and we'd almost die cracking ourselves up.

❧

WE STAYED IN A DUPLEX on the Saint Luke's Hospital compound. Travis and I liked to sit on the front porch and watch who the jeepneys would bring in. They rolled by all gussied up in shiny tassels and chrome ornaments, pinup girls and dashboard saints. They'd back up to the emergency entrance across the road, and Travis and I would try to guess what predicament brought the passengers here.

"Pregnant lady," I might say.

"Crazy man in a straight jacket," he'd counter.

Once we saw a boy arrive with the top part of a bowling pin stuck through his cheek. We'd have never guessed that could happen, not in a hundred years. Still, we watched scenes like this day after day, unaffected, the way we'd watch cartoons on TV, were we back in America.

On the day Mohammed Ali beat up Joe Frazier, the jeepneys arrived like an invading army.

"Bleedy head," Travis would say, and he'd almost always be right. Men got out, or got carried out, almost all of them bleeding profusely from cuts on their foreheads or under their eyes. Only time I got it right was when I called bloody nose or busted teeth, but Travis insisted that still counted as a bleedy head.

At last a jeepney pulled up on the near side of the road. Dad jumped out the back before it stopped. He clutched a sack to his chest.

"What's he bringing home this time?" I asked.

"Toys, I hope," Travis said. He was always losing his action figures and asking for more. I couldn't understand why. All he did was paint their faces dark purple and then promptly lose them.

Dad could hardly wait to show us what he'd brought home. He herded us inside and called for Mom, all the while clawing at the twine around the sack. When he finally got it out, I couldn't believe he'd get so excited over something so ugly. It was a mahogany carving that looked like an emaciated baby. Its head was too big for its body, and it had sad, curious eyes.

59

"It's a gift," Dad beamed, "from Mr. Golaz. He wanted to thank us for our plans to help his community."

Travis inspected the carving and said, "It looks all bony."

"Well, yes. I suppose it does," Dad agreed. "But if all goes according to our plan, we won't be seeing any more bony little boys and girls in that neighborhood."

"Maybe not," Mom said as she returned to the kitchen, "but you'll see a couple in this house if you don't start coming home in time for dinner. Now get in here. All of you."

Travis and I ran into the kitchen, followed by Dad. Travis asked him, before we sat down, why the sick people here rode to the hospital in jeepneys instead of ambulances. Dad started explaining something about President Marcos saving the ambulances for the army, but Mom interrupted: "You boys have been watching the emergency ward again?" And without waiting for a reply, she added, "I told you before I don't want you seeing that kind of thing."

Dad said, "Maybe it's good for the boys to see that kind of thing."

"They're too young to see that mess," Mom said.

Taking offence to her remark, I pointed out that I wasn't the one who woke up crying like a baby in the middle of the night.

"You're the baby," was Travis' clever retort.

"It's not mess," Dad said, raising his voice. "It's life."

"It's not right," Mom said, but she knew better than that. Keeping us ever mindful of the suffering of others was something that Dad prayed for every night.

She set a serving dish down on the table a little harder than usual. That's when we saw we were having fish again. The whole fish, eyes and all, on a bed of rice.

Travis pushed his plate away. "I can't eat that."

"You love fish," my mother reminded him.

"I don't like my dinner staring at me," he grumbled as he reached across the table to cover its eye. Dad slapped his hand away. "And I don't like it cold." Dad gave him that thin-ice look, but he pretended not to notice. "I'm sick of fish. I'm sick of this whole place. It really sucks."

I would be the first to admit that my little brother was a brat and the last to confess that he often said exactly what I was thinking.

60

"What did we do to get so poor?" he asked.

I knew he'd crossed a line somewhere when I saw red blotches spread across Dad's neck. "Poor?" he said. "I'll show you poor." He cocked his arm, ready to backhand Travis across the mouth, and at that moment, as if by some miracle, a gecko dropped from the ceiling. It wasn't your everyday gecko, either. This one was huge, the size of a banana, and it had translucent scales. I saw its veins and bones in action as it writhed across the table. Travis swiped it to the floor, along with his fork, knife and plate, then ran screaming into the bedroom.

Mom cocked her arm back, mimicking Dad with exaggerated gestures, and asked him, "How is this supposed to show him poor?"

Dad actually flinched, like she might really hit him.

~◎~

THAT NIGHT, with our room so quiet, I swear I could hear geckos climbing the walls. I prayed for it to stay this quiet, but I knew how busy the hospital was today. As soon as the last ray of light sank behind the compound walls, the noises began.

It started with the incinerator, which, by now, was filled with used bandages and anything else left over from the surgical rooms. The smell of it had already attracted every cat in the area to a feeding frenzy. I checked to make sure that my cat was still in the room because any minute now they would close the machine. A moment later I heard it start with a winding roar, and the howls of the cats trapped inside filled the air thicker than the smoke they soon became.

What came next was worse. After dark, the chambers in the mental ward echoed with similar cries, only the patients screamed about darkness and Jesus and needles.

Travis burrowed his face into his pillow and sobbed. I let him go on like that for a few minutes before asking him if he wanted to talk about it.

He said no, then asked me, "You remember last month, when we went to the beach?"

"Yeah."

"And that girl came up to us? And she gave us that huge shell?"

It was an amazing conch shell, glistening pink inside and orange like a tabby all over.

"Yeah."

"And she said it was a present from her father. She said he collected it from the bottom of the sea just for us."

"Yeah. So?"

"Well, I mean, how do you think he did that?"

I didn't know. We never met her father. But we'd seen him. He had no arms.

∽⊚∾

THE NEXT MORNING, as all mornings, the maid, Mrs. Golaz, woke up Travis and me with shouts of "*Magandang umaga!*" She tried to yank off our sheet, but we fought and screamed for it because we slept in our underwear. "Don't you touch us, you old witch!" Travis yelled. But she just laughed her strained cackle. She couldn't understand English. She clutched the sheet with her gnarled hand and snatched it away from us with strength that we thought was supernatural. Travis and I fled to the bathroom.

She'd come to Manila from Siquijor, an island known for its witchcraft, Dad had told us. And she had a pet monkey that she brought to our house once to show to Travis and me, but we were afraid to get near it, it looked so sick.

"That lady is gross," Travis said. "She wears the same stuff everyday and she smells like chickens. I don't know why Dad hired her."

I peered around the corner. "She's gone. Let's get dressed before she comes back."

∽⊚∾

FOR THE SECOND DAY STRAIGHT I went without ice cream. I thought I might die before dinner and couldn't understand why Mom wasn't cooking any. Then Dad came home with a storm in his eyes and I understood. He said something about Marcos razing slums again. We would be visiting the Golazes before their neighborhood got torn down. And without another word, he rounded up the whole family and marched us off the hospital compound to a crowded jeepney stand.

I didn't care for jeepneys, but Travis loved them, all their loud music and open air. Their chrome ornaments—horses and jets—looked like

62

toys to him. But this time, for the most part, he stared at a plastic Jesus swaying from the rear-view mirror and bearing the message: HE'S COUNTING ON US. He asked Mom: "Does that mean he's counting on us, like all of us? Or is that U-S, like United States?"

Dad and I looked away like we didn't hear that, and we hoped no one understood him, but turned heads and raised eyebrows indicated otherwise.

"That means all of us," Mom whispered.

Dad passed a few pesos to the driver and we jumped out as the jeepney rolled away. He led us through a crowd of vendors selling overripe guava and papaya, past a few bulldozers, and into a maze of shacks that were tacked together with scrap wood, cardboard and tarp.

Travis complained about the smell of burning garbage and chickens and pee, and about the fact that everyone was staring at us. They'd perched themselves on posts, stumps, or anywhere they could find room. Their skin was tight on their ribs and spines; some looked like they had beetles crawling up their backbones. They kept their knees pulled up behind their ears and watched us like vampire bats. A teenager wearing nothing but ragged blue jeans threw loops of rubber-coated wire on a bed of coals. It burst into flames and billowed out thick black smoke that rose and blended in with the dark clouds behind him.

Above all they looked dangerous, but I figured we were safe. Dad knew the area, and police sirens were always near since Marcos declared martial law.

The path wound through alleys downhill to a dead end and a decaying cement structure. We stopped a good ten feet short of the front doorway, which was open or lacked a door. Inside, four children played quietly while their father crouched next to an oil lamp. He hacked and whittled at a black log, and smiled as a face emerged from the wood. Next to him, Mrs. Golaz fixed a vacant gaze on her husband's hands.

Travis yelled: "Mrs. Golaz!" And he ran toward her waving his hands like he hadn't seen her in a month. "Mrs. Golaz! *Halo! Magandang umaga!*"

I thought: What an idiot. It's near dark and he's shouting 'good morning' at Mrs. Golaz.

She looked up, her face spreading in a big familiar grin. She started to stand, but then hesitated as though frozen in a horrific thought. She turned and hissed at her kids. They scrambled to put away their toys, but it was too late. We'd seen them, the action figures. Superman, Aquaman, G.I. Joe—all with faces painted dark purple.

Mom leaned over to Dad. "Were we invited?" she whispered through a clenched smile. "Or are you just trying to show us poor?"

He told us to wait outside while he talked to Mr. Golaz. The alley dimmed as clouds above thickened. The men chatted in the doorway. Mr. Golaz stood in the center of the frame, hands positioned against either side. When the first few drops of rain fell, he urged us to hurry back to the main road.

About the time we returned to where the jeepney dropped us off, thunder crashed through the sky and sheets of rain came slashing down. The jeepneys filled up fast. There was always room for one more, but not one would take a family of four.

We ran for blocks before we found a place to take cover. A neon sign above the door said MANILA SIRENS. We huddled into a red vinyl booth. Two hostesses wearing black bikinis arrived with a menu. Dad's face blanched when he looked at it. He slapped it shut and ordered a few sticks of satay, fried plantains, and a round of orange soda. Near the bar, a woman in a yellow bikini sang "Tie a Yellow Ribbon" to an otherwise empty room. She sang with giddy passion and almost sounded American.

We waited there for hours, just listening to the singer and the storm. A short man in a baby-blue tuxedo kept our drinks fresh. He seemed friendly enough, laughing as he asked Travis and me, "Do you enjoy my chicks?" And his apologetic tone sounded genuine when he told us we had to leave.

Dad looked up. "We can't leave in this," he said, gesturing upward, as if the rain were falling through the ceiling.

"But you must," the man insisted. "We're closed now."

Dad checked his watch. It was past 11:30.

"Martial law. Curfew is in half an hour," the man said as he escorted us to the door.

Dad told us to wait in the doorway and then ran into the street, waving his arms wildly at an oncoming cab. It blew its horn as it splashed by. Its wake rocked the debris floating down the sidewalk. Newspaper, cardboard, a detergent bottle—a little armada of garbage sailed away.

Dad pulled what must've been two or three hundred pesos from his pocket and waved the bills at the next cab. It stopped. He opened the door and waved us over. "Hold hands," he shouted. When we hesitated, he yelled at me: "Hold your brother's hand and don't let go until you get in the cab!"

Mom seized my elbow and dug her nails in. I grabbed Travis' wrist and pulled him into the flooded street. I thought I heard him whisper, "*Foo-shee!*" But when I turned to look, he wasn't laughing. Fear and rain filled his eyes. He looked ready to cry.

"People here are thieves," Dad said as we piled into the back seat. "They'll steal anything." I didn't know if he was talking about Travis' toys or the taxi driver insisting on such a high fare. But then I understood when he said, "That boy you saw, the one burning the wire. That was a telephone line he stole right off the pole. He was burning off the insulation so that he could sell the copper wire inside."

He wiped the rain from his face and added: "They'll steal grates off storm drains and covers off manholes, and they'll sell it all as scrap metal." He didn't sound like he was blaming them or passing judgment, but rather explaining, almost apologetically, why he ordered us to hold hands before running into the street.

By 11:50 the army jeeps were on patrol, but the driver sped on with one eye on the road and the other on the soggy bills. A minute to midnight, guards let us through the compound gates. We were safe at home, but I wondered where the driver would go. Travis, always sharing my thoughts out loud, asked Dad if the driver could stay with us, just for the night. Dad said no and hurried us into the house.

Later, just as I was falling asleep, I heard the siren of an ambulance. I dreamt it was coming here, to St. Luke's, with Joe Frazier on the gurney. He asked me if he should pay me back for all the ice cream money I lost betting on him. His face was so bashed up, all purple and lumpy, I could hardly stand to look at him. I turned away and told him no, he probably needed it more.◆

Curt Rode

EDINBURGH ELEGY

for David O. White (1966-1994)

His mother's friends
Promised her they'd release
A film cannister of his ashes
Near Arthur's Seat,
Where I took his picture
Sitting at the top
On the brass marker that gives
The direction and distance
To places we'd been,
Or hoped to go.

Should I love one place more
Than Loch Lomond or Stranraer,
Now that he's part
Of its pollen and dirt?

I don't know;
I'm as new to this
Tide of grief
As I was to the city
We climbed above
As it rained without conviction,
Thin clouds of mist
Folding in from the firth.

Margaret Pennycook

DUST AND ASHES

Don't look for me
in the wrong places.
I shall not molder in a grave.
My flesh will not wither
my bones bleach brittle.
No future fossil hunter
shall expose my history.
No one can preserve,
wrap, or mummify me
beneath a pyramid.
I do not lie dismembered
under the remains of girders and walls
among still-smoldering fires
or smoke
scented with burnt entrails.

I float on the wind
above the East River
and the Hudson
catching for a moment on Liberty's torch.
I rush past the tourists
watching from the top
of the Empire State Building
and over the Art Deco temple curves
of the Chrysler Building.
I swirl round Lincoln Center
rising on the high notes

like a seagull on a thermal.
Above Central Park,
I linger by Strawberry Fields.
Oh, John,
when I sang at a candlelight vigil
for you
could I
imagine
the wicks flickering for my own violent end?

No more rushed Styrofoam cups of coffee
No more tuna and bean sprouts for lunch
No more staying late at the office
or nervous journeys on the late train.
No more pretending
he isn't there,
the man with long hair
and ragged blue coat
who slept in the Towers' shadows.
No more time to worry about
Mom's Alzheimer's
or the results of the mammogram.
No need to starve for
that dress in Macy's window.
It wouldn't have suited me anyway.
And the girls' recitals
will go on without me,
but then they often did.

We come from dust and ashes
and to them we all return
but I thought it would take time.
Time for hair to grey, memory to fail
arthritis to set in.
Time for bones and flesh to age
to rot
before disintegration.

As it is,
inhaled by ventilation systems
in the Russian Tea Room, the Majestic Theater
and the Plaza
vented out of corner delis, nail parlors and jazz
clubs
sucked into the tunnels of the subway
at 42nd Street and Times Square
and, felled by rain, to gush and gurgle
through the gutters
of Broadway and Fifth Avenue
I streak the early snow
fleck your Donna Karan suits
stick to your Nike sneakers
scatter in your hair, sting your eyes, and scour
your lungs.

So, don't dig for fragments and splinters.
My essence is no longer framed
by their constraints
or those of past and present.
Whether the city shimmers and flashes
beneath dark clouds
or gleams
under a blue, blue sky
look for me in its future.

Emily Dewhirst

How My Grandparents
Created a Nomad

*I*t wasn't my fault I became a nomad with an ever increasing addiction to adventurous travel. It was the fault of my grandparents. For my high school graduation present they gave me money for educational travel. So in 1947 at seventeen years of age, I chose to bicycle through Europe for three months, and I spent an extra three weeks working at a refugee shelter in Cauterets in the French Pyrenees Mountains.

From my early days I was curious about other cultures, drawn to people who spoke different languages. But without doubt I would have trod the normal path of young people my age if I hadn't spent an eye-opening summer in France, Belgium and Switzerland just after World War II. I found myself in a world I had no preparation to meet.

The American Youth Hostel Association, the organizer of the trip, cautioned participants to have multiple-speed bikes. I had no bicycle, and new ones were barely back in production. However, my father talked the Schwinn Company into shipping what they had, a beautiful black one-speed complete with tool kit, pump and spare tire. I was too excited to realize how difficult it would be to bike over mountains on a one-speed.

I was a strange sight as I boarded first the *Zephyr* then the *Empire Builder*, crack luxury trains of the '40s, setting out alone on the thirty hour train ride from Minneapolis to New York. I had my saddle bags over one shoulder, a sleeping bag and a bike basket filled with tools and a portable cooking apparatus on the other, and a spare tire draped over my head. I staggered under the load, for I had clothes and rain coverings, cooking and eating utensils, and food: sugar, coffee, powdered milk, canned goods. There were severe shortages and food rationing at that time in Europe, and we were to bring our own provisions so we would not impose. The population was still trying to find food, refashion lives out of the chaos of bombed cities, locate separated family members, cope with the recent deaths of so many, and resolve in their minds the treachery and perfidy of both invaders and even some neighbors.

In New York I stayed alone at the Hotel Times Square for two nights, and on the morning of departure I met our group. We were three boys and seven girls, ranging in age from seventeen to thirty. Edna, a woman in her thirties, was our leader. She looked competent, but looks can deceive, as they did in this case. Two of the girls, Marion and Faith, were my age but in their senior years at the University of Chicago, obviously intelligent but lacking common sense. My favorite was Sue, a Nebraska girl, quiet, self-assured and dependable.

After the meeting we undertook a harrowing dash through New York City to get Spanish visas, which we never used, barely making it to the ship on time, only to sit all afternoon because the sailing was delayed for lack of crew. We waited, not knowing whether our trip would begin and end simultaneously in New York or go on as expected. Finally, enough volunteer sailors appeared, and the red and white flag was hoisted, meaning we had a full crew and a pilot to guide us out of the harbor.

We sailed on the *Marine Marlin*, a troop ship leased by the Navy to various youth groups and displaced people returning home. Troop ships are utilitarian, not luxurious. My sleeping quarters were in the bowels of the ship, far under the surface of the ocean. I found myself in a vast space filled with hundreds of canvas hammocks suspended on chains in tiers four deep. I chose an upper bunk inches from the metal side of the ship so I could hear the water. True, the drainpipes were also there, but I preferred to think of the waves. It took some odd maneuvering to get in my hammock without cracking my head or stepping on a face or leg. The drainpipes took most of the room on the only free side. I would swing up on the pipes, duck my head at just the right time before it collided with the main steel tubing and hope to land in the hammock. Getting down was another matter. I would do a jackknife dive, feet first, and slide down between the suspended bunks and the pipes. The space was barely wide enough to squeeze through if I held my breath. I didn't dare put on weight during the eleven day voyage. Since no room existed to dress or undress in between the rows of bunks, I struggled in and out of my clothes while prone, my nose almost touching the ceiling. We spent our time on board attending language, history and culture classes, but at night we bundled on deck and told stories and sang and watched the stars dance in the sky.

Docking in Antwerp early one morning, we waited on the cobblestone quay for our bikes to be unloaded. Overhead were enormous signs, *Verboden te Rooken*: forbidden to smoke. Dust clouds swirled around us as hefty Belgian women wielding enormous straw brooms swept the cobblestones and horse drawn carts with huge wooden wheels jostled over the uneven floor. To our horror, we saw our bikes coming over the side of the ship, strung together through their front braces by a large rope. The crane jerked them about, smashing them against the keel. The incredible damage took all day to fix. So it was late afternoon before we pushed off for the Antwerp hostel, following our leader, Edna, through the town, her black skirt flapping around her ankles, threatening to get entangled in the spokes of her bike.

White helmeted policemen, sturdy bicycles and street cafes with brightly striped awnings of orange, blue and green crowded Antwerp. We passed women in wooden shoes scrubbing doorsteps, beautiful iron grill work, abandoned shells left from bombed buildings, hastily rebuilt homes and open spaces where buildings once stood.

The two University of Chicago girls, Marion and Faith, barely hung on at the end of our cavalcade, obviously lacking in biking experience. This was an omen for the entire trip. Marion had no physical prowess or coordination, only big dark eyes which preyed on the kindness of young men who regularly fell at her feet, eager to help. Her friend Faith quickly caught on to the tactics.

Thankfully we didn't put the wheels to the road every day. Often we punctuated our trip with sightseeing and sometimes took the train to gobble up the miles we would have labored over.

People from all over Europe filled the Antwerp hostel. They cooked, cleaned and sang. We joined them and had our first experience with international living and working together. That night in the girls' dorm, I watched a German girl strip off her clothes, take two wire brushes and beat her body until I was sure she would bring blood. I asked her why she did that, and she replied that in the Hitler Youth Camp, she was taught this was good for her health.

The next day I realized our group was in trouble. We had non-bikers and a leader who was always lost and who had strong individual ideas of where to go and what to see. At the start of our first day of biking, two people had flat tires. Edna sketched a vague map and told us to go on to the Brussels hostel fifty two kilometers away. Staying together was impossible because some had five- speed bikes, others had three and I had one. Two of us separated from the group and wandered through town looking for the Brussels highway, almost getting run over by the tramways which swung from the middle of the street into the curb. They looked like Toonerville Trolleys, and during rush hour several were hitched together, lurching down the street like a runaway train. We all got lost by ones or twos, and in trying to find our way, I think we covered every lane and highway between Antwerp and Brussels. Eventually we all straggled into the hostel, except Edna, who was lost until late at night.

༺꙳༻

Diary Entry July 7, 1947
I am sitting on a ledge overlooking a dam in the city of Metz, France. It is a quarter to nine and already dark. Sue and I had devoured our sandwiches late, so we volunteered to watch the bikes while the others went to eat. We are to wait for Edna, Marion, and Faith who are missing, of course.

༺꙳༻

LATER, no one came. We went to the hostel, waiting and worrying until almost midnight when a Belgian boy carrying a hostel sign told us that the two missing girls were at the train station. There we found them surrounded by adoring Belgian boys. We were then escorted to another hostel in town, not on our leader's map, where we found Edna asleep, totally unconcerned about anyone.

We took the train to Luxembourg City the next day. Total confusion. One of the bikes was at the wrong station, so Edna stayed behind, forgetting to dole out the sandwiches. The trip was fun, regardless, for a group of French boys helped drag our bikes and equipment from one end of the platform to the other and sang to us until they got off at a small town. While the train was still in the station, one of the boys ran back and forth, giving us the cheese sandwiches from his group's pack. His friends did not think too much of their disappearing lunch, so to distract this generous boy, they opened his suitcase, taking out each article of his belongings, and lined them up about a foot apart along the platform.

Our separateness continued, as the group simply could not stay together with our different ideas of what we wanted to see and our different needs for biking time. One night, five of us arrived in Lausanne, Switzerland, and decided to leave our heavy packs at the hostel and push on to Montreux to see the castle of Chillon where Byron wrote his famous poem "The Prisoner of Chillon." The scenery was breathtaking. Snow-covered mountains overlooked our steep road which, in turn, overlooked the lake. We approached the town at dark. Along the lake a row of weeping willows, bathed in flickering blue-green lights, dipped their branches into the water. Graceful swans, tinted blue by the lights, swam under the trees. As we turned a bend, the huge castle rose out of the water, its turrets and towers awash in brilliant white spotlights. Wanting to sleep near the cell of the famous prisoner, we spread out our sleeping bags in the castle gardens. One of the boys protested that it was too public, so we moved to a spot a few feet off a mountain road. In the morning we were surprised to find ourselves on the path to the Lord Byron Tea Room, and people were arriving for breakfast. No privacy at all for getting dressed.

I discovered while biking over hills with the sun beating down that my pack was unbearably heavy. During the rest of the trip, I dotted the roads with my belongings and learned to live with less. Even my spare tire was abandoned somewhere in France. However, our legs did get stronger as they became conditioned to the pedaling. I had never had slim legs or ankles, but on the trip they became like sturdy posts of wood. Many roads were in poor condition, and we bounced over potholes and groaned in agony due to extreme fatigue. Occasionally, there were blue skies and cooler weather, but the scenery was always spectacular and the people curious and friendly.

Getting sick happened frequently, and it was very inconvenient. Dysentery is tolerable when you are at home with a toilet nearby. It is impossible on a bike trip. Woods would not materialize when needed, washing clothes was not possible, and biking was out of the question with the weakness. Sometimes we left a sick person at a hostel to catch up later by train. Sometimes someone offered to stay with him or her and proceed slowly. The only remedy available for bouts of dysentery was the tincture of opium we had been advised to carry with us.

Apart from our few days in Switzerland, our daily diet consisted of heavy dark bread and jam, sometimes with a tomato or cheese. Edna held the group money, and we took turns shopping and making sandwiches in the morning, eating them as we biked our separate ways. At night, if and when we ever met each other, we had more bread and jam. When staying in a hostel, we used our sterno cooking equipment to heat water for coffee and occasionally soup, depending on what we could find along the road.

From Geneva we veered west, biking through the Jura Mountains toward Lyons, France, then down along the Rhone River. During the war, I had sent care packages to a French family living in the Drome River Valley. I realized we were only thirty miles from their home and decided to take a side trip to see them. One of the boys went with me. We biked all afternoon, slept in a field of sunflowers and reached the medieval town of Crest by midmorning. We were unable to find the family, but with the help of the townspeople, we discovered they lived in the tiny silk factory town of Bertholet, another ten miles further.

The Boissys could not believe I had appeared out of nowhere. We spent the afternoon visiting the factory, meeting the silk workers in town and seeing the considerable war damage, for this was an area where the Resistance had been active. The Boissy apartment was in a building dating back to the 1700's, with a stand up toilet in the hall, one flight down. They lived with a grandfather who was in his nineties, a veteran of *la Grande Guerre*, World War I. The family kept insisting we eat, but knowing how little they had, we refrained, saying we had just eaten (but in truth, that was the day before). M. Boissy played his violin for us. Mme. Boissy, pregnant at the time, named her baby after me, and this warm, loving family became a part of my life forever.

The rest of the trip was a blur of heat, Mediterranean sand and remains of Roman aqueducts and theaters, medieval towns and castles. After three months of biking, we were somewhere southwest of Carcassonne, that spectacular medieval double walled city. We had only a day's ride left to reach our work project in the Pyrenees, but I was exhausted and experiencing waves of nausea and diarrhea. Some of us had slept in the rain by the side of the road, but at 4 a.m. I was unable to take any more. I left a note and biked toward the camp at Cauterets in the cool of the early morning, thinking I would either make it or die somewhere along the road. By mid-morning I rode into a small village, and while washing my face in the town fountain, I saw a miniscule white pastry truck drew up. The driver, a middle-aged, dapper Frenchman, asked me where I was going and if I would like a ride. It was a case of desperation, and I accepted his offer to let me off in the town where our paths would part. I had second thoughts during the trip, however, as he began patting my bare leg where my shorts ended. Thankfully it went no further, and his kindness put me out of the misery of hours of biking, giving me the courage to forge on to Cauterets where I arrived around noon, far ahead of the others.

At the work project, we were to help rebuild an ancient stone barn as a center for refugee children who had lost their parents during the war. Thirty to forty people from England, Ireland, Denmark, and Italy always drifted in and out. One Scotsman wore a full kilt. I was given a plate of food, and I sat down at a long table filled with Danes, big, husky and very blond. My Swedish ancestry helped me wade through the language tangle. After lunch the English engineer, Vincent, head of the project, and his assistant, a Dane named Magnus, gave me a tour of the mountainside camp. Conditions were primitive. The mess hall was in the bottom of the stone barn and had an uneven loose rock and gravel floor. The girls slept on straw mattresses on the rickety boards of the loft, and the boys had tents up on the mountainside. The washing place was a plank with basins near the edge of a mountain stream with ice cold glacier water.

Breakfast consisted of porridge, compliments of the English group, black bread and tea. Lunch was cooked by the housefather, "Touta," so named as a child because he ate everything in sight. We usually ate bean or lentil soup made with the leftover porridge, some tomatoes and potatoes. Supper was warmed up leftovers from lunch with extra potatoes and sometimes stringy meat. The French bread was wartime bread, mixed with various grains and we suspected other things, like sawdust.

Touta was the camp character: a comic, a communist, an atheist, engaged to an American Quaker. Touta was always "going to catch grasshoppers," his expression for a trip to the toilet made of two holes with a board between them. Others took a "pilgrimage to Rome." In any case we did both frequently, for something in the water made these trips necessary.

Assignments were rotated, but I was often put on sand washing because transport involved hauling heavy cement sacks up the mountain on a wooden cart, too strenuous for most of the girls. The object was to pour a concrete floor in the barn. Concrete is made of cement and sand, but there is little sand in the Pyrenees and it is expensive. Therefore we dug a hole, set up a pulley system to send the dirt down to the camp and sifted it through a wire screen to remove the rocks. After washing what was left, the sand sank to the bottom of the trough, was put in buckets and hauled back up by pulley where it was mixed with water and cement.

In the evening after work, we would hike to the nearest village to *the Casino*, a small outdoor café, where we danced and sang. Sometimes the boys of the ski school in town invited us for a "sing song." In summer they were mountain guides for visitors who intended to climb the highest mountain in the Pyrenees, the Vignemal.

Each weekend at our camp, the experienced climbers made an attempt to reach the peak of the Vignemal. It was a two day climb; we slept on ice and rocks and roping over a treacherous glacier. Climbers rarely reached the top because of bad fog or rain. The first weekend I watched the group get ready with their backpacks, sleeping bags, food, spiked boots, ropes and ice axes. I wanted so much to go. They did not reach the top. Magnus, one of the best climbers, assured me he would make it possible. He borrowed boots for me and carried my pack on top of his. He knew how strenuous those two days would be, and I had never climbed a mountain before. He also tied me in the middle of a rope with himself at one end and an experienced English climber on the other. The eight others in the group were tied together on one rope, but they were seasoned climbers. On the climb up the mountain, we met one of the ski school boys coming down, his bloody hands held in front of him. A French climber in his party had slipped into a crevasse while roping over the glacier. They had tried to pull her out, but they had been unable to do so because the fissure was narrow and deep, twisting and turning. She died somewhere within the glacier. That really frightened me, but I couldn't turn back.

I was exhausted after the first day's climb, and the bitter cold night was worse. We started again at dawn, roping over the glacier with its strange blue cracks. Finally, we climbed over dangerous boulders and loose rock and reached the top. I was too paralyzed to even look around me. Going down was worse, but Magnus wisely tied me to an end of the rope and let me down first. As I would slip, he would let me dangle until I found my footing. Never again would I try anything so difficult and frightening. The recompense was that the boys in the ski school who didn't believe I could make it to the top feted me with a party and a gift of the ice axe we used, carved with my name, the mountain, the date and the elevation. I was the first American girl to make it to the top that summer.

Saying goodbye to all my close friends at the camp was difficult; although in the years to come, we became even closer. When Magnus died fifteen years ago, it was one of the saddest days of my life.

Our group headed to Lourdes where we took the train to Paris. The hostel, a tent camp in the center of the city, was overflowing, so Sue and I were sent to a seedy hotel where I had my first experience with bed bugs. But Paris is another story.

I was never able to let go of my 1947 experience. Not two years later I was on a ship going back to Paris where I studied at the Sorbonne, later worked as a tri-lingual interpreter in Italy, then a stewardess with Pan American Airways. I always found a way to deepen the attachment I had with friends all over Europe and beyond.

Realizing how much my bicycle trip had opened my eyes to the world,

I spent many years taking private groups of students to Europe. I also lived in Denmark, motorcycled to the Arctic Circle, rode camels in Egypt and India and as an educational specialist, worked in Africa, the Middle East, the Far East, Central Asia and South America. In my sixties, I went to Kazakhstan for two and a half years with the Peace Corps and returned one spring to Central Asia to see friends and help train English teachers in the schools.

This lifelong wanderlust was triggered by a high school graduation gift from grandparents who never dreamed where it would lead. I have never truly come back from the moon.◆

Barbara Crooker

And

One week later, and
I need to see my mother,
upstate New York, far
from the center, the devastation,
but the need to be with her is strong,
so I get in the car and drive north,
and my best friend from high school
goes to see her parents, too, and we meet
for lunch. And Mom cries when Judy leaves,
then we both cry when I leave,
and then I'm on the Thruway
and I need gas, and I start talking
to the woman at the next pump,
and by the time we replace
the nozzles, we're crying
and wishing each other
safe journey home and no one knows
what's coming next, the darkness is gathering,
thick as crows in a roosting tree,
but still, there's an and—

BLUE COLOR REMEMBRANCES
by Catie Tappan

Keith Flynn

LEFT BEHIND

12-24-99

This jejune Jesuit and myself,
Pure joist, a beam balanced beneath
Our bottle, scotch warm in my throat
As we share conversation and a limo
From LaGuardia to the snowy West side.
God is barely alive, he confesses,
And time is short, but scotch is
Better than port. I don't know,
I answer, I'm a whisky man myself,
But if forced to simile I would state
Unequivocally that God is like a tractor
And the rapture a myth in the way
Of his corn. Yes, he says, Jesus
Was to mortal woman born,
Homeless and naked as a thief,
Stealing what little warmth the animals
Provided. I'm divided, I admit,
Staring behind the joint I've lit
Through the smoke to the harbor
And its horn, ramming Manhattan with snow.
Those who read the Bible know, my friend
Continues, that the signposts point
Toward a glorious end, earthquakes and
Hurricanes, pestilence, the Earth a shrike
Of a house, waiting to explode. Ah but
Not before he calls the faithful home,

Right? I ask. Not until, the minister gloats,
Not until the earthly vessels float to meet
The King on high. I'm nigh to floating
As well, with twenty more minutes to ride,
Trapped in a limo with a minister
From Memphis and feeling left behind.
The poor are easy targets, I decide,
For they will never ride in chariots
Or drink cognac from a golden chalice,
So to pray for the mighty to fall
Is, all in all, their only defense. I sense
In my companion a rumbling, a personal
Recollection of one of the prominent
People he has known, but instead he moans,
Light-headed from my secondhand smoke,
And says simply, the devil is no joke.
Well what's the devil to do at the century's
End, except to sing the scarecrow blues
And trawl the alley for friends.
I'll pray for your soul, the preacher
Replies, but this is my building and I
Must say good-bye. He gives my hand
A long warm shake, and then waiting
For the silence to break, I knock on the
Window and the driver stops. The Jesuit
Rocks, then stumbles, leaving tracks in the snow,
And I wonder how long the wind will blow,
And I realize at the same time
That I'd been stiffed and the fare
From the airport is mine alone.
I laugh and toke, pondering my Xmas
Gift, serenaded by a Jesuit who
Needed a lift, a half-bottle of scotch
And a warning for a tip. The black
Car rips a trail through the lights.
God is a tractor, plowing long into the night.

Jenny Brooks White

SPECULATION
Ikoma, Japan, 1999

In a Japanese bookstore
I bought a map of Tennessee
and hung it on the wall
of my tiny apartment.

Names like *Bells*,
Friendship, *Finger* reminded me
of cotton gins, back yards, and oak trees.
Highways I once drove down
took me to *Milan*, *Paris*, *Memphis*.

I looked for *Cherokee*,
Bird Song, and *Cub Creek* along
the thin blue line, but the places
where my grandfather and I thrived
on trot lines, crappie rigs, and six dozen minnows
were unnamed oxbows and tributaries.

With no *Hatchie River* to lead me home,
the *Forked Deer River* ran close.
But *Smokey Lane* wasn't there,
Miss Gladys' pond gone,
Gum Flat not even mentioned.
I was lost in a map of home
where my grandfather's land
was shapeless, my house
only a speculation.

Jeannette Brown

Seeing Through Water

He thinks we're going fly-fishing. Actually, this trip is to buy time while I decide what to do about his recent marriage proposal. I am middle-aged and wary of romantic misadventures.

I should mention that Jack is very attractive and that he accompanied his proposal with a rather huge marquise-cut diamond. The ring does not accompany us on this trip.

I have never been fly-fishing. We buy a new reel for his ancient fly rod, last used in his college days. At the surplus store we buy vests with pockets and plastic rain ponchos and rubber booties, which, Jack assures me, will keep us from slipping and sliding on the river rocks.

We are going from Austin, Texas to Cody, Wyoming. He thinks we should drive. Three days up, two days fishing, and three days back. I am skeptical of this schedule.

It is July and we're in Amarillo when the air conditioner goes out, so we roll down the windows and are attacked by a swarm of huge black flies that ride with us out of Texas and into New Mexico. Three of them make it to Colorado.

On the drive, Jack entertains me by telling our future. Futures. We can be hippies in Taos. We can be swells in New York. We can be artistic in Austin or dramatic in Marin County. The mind boggles. Of course, he includes the option of just being ourselves. It's up to me. I commit to, "We'll see." No need to rush into something that might later be regretted.

Except for Jack's fantasies, the trip up is numbing: a dozen hours of beautiful scenery, then a motel. At rest stops and greasy spoons, my body buzzes with the vibration of the pickup's engine. After two days I get excited when we stop for the night in Cheyenne. It's only 6 pm. As I help haul our suitcases, gear, and coolers from the pickup into the motel, I think about putting on something silky to wear to dinner. Maybe we'll linger over a final glass of red wine, relaxing in romance. Jack spreads the map across the bed, tracking the trip. He discovers we have barely crossed the state line into Wyoming. We want to be in Casper, not Cheyenne, although you can see how he could make that mistake with the Cs and all. Casper is hundreds of miles to the north. He explains our dilemma to the motel clerk while we take the suitcases, gear, and coolers back out to the pickup. He leaves a twenty on the dresser. We drive for hours, stopping only for a burger-to-go.

Cody, Wyoming is a rustic little town, except that today is the 3rd of July—rodeo time—so the streets are full of tourists and cowboys. Solitude on the Snake River sounds inviting.

We arrange to meet our guide, Bruce, at 7 a.m. at his store. I didn't realize he'd have a store. He explains that the booties we bought are useless—we need real boots with funny felt soles. And we need flies with boxes to keep them in. And Jack needs a special pair of sunglasses that will allow him to see through the water. And we need all kinds of other gear that add up to about $350.

Jack and I drive our pickup to the designated spot where Bruce picks us up and loads our gear into his Explorer. On the drive to the Snake, Bruce lays out our day: we'll take a few casting lessons, put in the raft, float a little ways down the river, fish awhile, float awhile, have lunch, fish, float, fish, float, etc., until about 5 p.m.

We leave the road and cut back through brush for about a mile, parking on a spot where the land runs into the water. On the other side is the twenty-foot wall of the river's gorge. It is a glorious sunny day, warming up now that it's 8:30. Jack decides that we don't need our surplus store rain ponchos or jackets.

As we're putting the raft in, Bruce mentions that several weeks ago he guided two women. He says they caught a lot of fish, but they didn't help him with the chores. I think this is a gender slam, but I make a mental note to be helpful. Jack does not. He believes that hired-help should not need help.

The Snake River is not deep, wide, muddy and dark like the rivers in Texas. We'd call this a stream. Here it's about a foot deep, moving, swirling so that leaves and small fish spin end-over-end as they drift by. The water reflects the sun one instant, lets you see below the next, like a strobe light in a bad bar. Underneath are jagged rocks and sandy patches. The river is noisy, but rhythmic and calming. I think about a nap.

On the shore, Bruce shows us how to cast. Jack moves down river. I cast, catching Bruce's hat on the backswing. This has happened to him so many times that he doesn't flinch, but he does back off to give me more room.

We get into the raft and Bruce assigns seats. Jack and I are in the front, casting into the breeze. My casts are not graceful because I am terrified that I will catch Bruce again. He must not realize this because he keeps giving me instructions, pretty much the same ones over and over. Jack gets the hang of it and instructs me, too.

We float to a bend in the Snake and get out. Bruce and I drag the raft to the shore. Jack does not help.

Stepping into the water wakes me up. It's only six inches deep, but it tries to push me over even after I have found my footing. The icy water seeps slowly into my boots, feeling good/bad like wetting my pants.

I am lulled into the motion of casting. The river is moving right to left and I am casting south to north. The grace of the line is awesome, making patterns in the air then repeating them on top of the water. It reminds me of a million moving infinity symbols or the shape of the IUD I used to wear.

Jack's rod is not so much ancient as it is irrelevant—three pieces of two different rods, which tend to fly in different directions when he casts. Bruce has top-of-the-line stuff. He loans Jack his rod. (I could make Jack laugh with a few lewd jokes about men and their rods, but I'm sure Bruce has heard them all and my relationship with him is already strained.) This leaves Bruce nothing to fish with, so he 'helps' me, holding onto my rod as I cast. Suddenly, there is a fish on the end of my line, but I'm not sure who caught it.

Jack was born to fly-fish. He has no time to practice his cast because he's always taking a fish off the line. He doesn't lose flies. He understands how to bite the line and tie on a new fly (he insists on trying each of the dozen we have bought from Bruce). Of course, he can see through water and I can't.

When it's time for lunch, Bruce pulls food and a camping table with seats from the raft. I help him drag the cooler ashore. Jack goes for a walk.

I am a little surprised about the food. It is not manly food—jerky and mustard and white bread—but deli food—potato salad, salami and other delicacies—purchased that morning on Bruce's way into meet us. But it is tasty and we have M&Ms for dessert. Jack takes another walk while Bruce and I clean up.

We have spent all morning in the same bend. Bruce seems a little surprised as he announces that we are supposed to be much further down the river by now. We are to fish from the raft, so we can get back on schedule.

The Snake River is catch and release. You can't cook the fish for dinner; you can't take them home. Because our guide knows this part of the river, he knows which fish lives in which hole. He tells Jack to cast into that little pool behind the bush. Jack does, and catches Mr. Gills. (My opinion of Bruce softens a little.) So we stop and take it off the hook and take its picture and throw it back. Because Jack is such an excellent fisherman, we do not progress down the river. Jack hits every pool; the fish hit every cast. The repetition is boring. We are deep into the gorge; I cannot see the sun or a tree or any land that is not vertical. It's a post-card perfect place and I wish I could rid myself of the feeling that we are about to be swallowed by something.

Catching fish is boring, except for one. Jack catches the fish and throws it into the raft for its photo session. A bush snags Bruce's $500 rod. The skinny third of the pole stays with the bush as we keep floating, letting out the fishing line until it has draped twenty feet of riverside. Bruce flies into action, jumping into the water to stop the raft, taking the fish off the line, throwing it into the water, running onto the bank after his rod. Jack is very calm in the face of his potential purchase of a new, but damaged fly rod. But Bruce saves the fish and the rod and we float down the river again.

Bruce is frustrated with me as a student. Perhaps I am his only failure. Jack instructs, too. Fishing comes so easily he doesn't understand how anyone could not get it. I am getting a little fed up with both of them.

In fact, I'm very fed up. We are still not progressing down the river. Sleeper and Sam Boy and Big 'Un and Old Man and all the other trout are lying just beneath the surface, ready to strike. And we must stop for each of them.

As we round a bend, the weather changes instantly. The sky is black and the temperature drops 10 degrees. It begins to sprinkle. Bruce mentions a predicted storm, speculates on how fast it is rolling in, tries to assure us that we can beat it. He is genuinely concerned. So am I. Jack is not.

We are on a river in a gorge with walls too steep to climb. It beginnings to rain. And the temperature continues to drop. I am cold and wet. A storm is coming. And still these two men will not pass up one hole, one pool, one fish. It's possible that Jack has caught ninety percent of the fish that live in the Snake River, yet he will not pull in his rod, and Bruce will not put the raft into high gear. Of course, there is no gear except Bruce, who is rowing.

I do not whine, I do not bitch. I do not make demands. But I'm considering it. Intuitively, Bruce pulls a plastic windbreaker from under his seat and offers it to me. And more M&Ms.

The wind whips up, not quite to a roar, but impressive. The raindrops are huge. My lips are blue. My nose is running. I have crossed the line from unlovely to repulsive, both visually and spiritually. Jack is still casting. I quit thinking about how miserable I am and begin to think about dying. Dying in a river in Wyoming where I probably won't be found until I've lain in the water for three days and the frogs have gnawed out my eyeballs and eaten the tender skin off my swollen lips and the fish are nesting in my hair.

I will die in the company of two men I loathe. Two maniacal, egotistical, insensitive men who would rather die—literally—than miss a catch. If I live, I will not enter into this marriage, this merger with a man who would put me in danger. If this peaceful river ride has turned into a life-threatening situation, imagine the rest of my life with him—safaris, mountain climbing, hang gliding—an endless list of ways to almost die.

I will live. I might have a small, predictable life, but it will be a life.

Back in the motel room, wrapped in every towel and blanket I can find, I massage my nose back to life while I explain my fury to Jack. "But

Hon," he replies, "I knew we'd be okay." He's stunned that that does-n't make me feel better. Sensing that he is losing ground, he holds me tight, rocking me gently, whispering a list of gourmet dinners he'll make in our new kitchen.

In the icy silence of the drive back to Texas, I can't breathe right. I heave sighs from the sadness of being in love with a maniac. I am the three-day Queen of Tragedy.

Near Amarillo, I start watching for the black flies. It's Saturday, nearly sunset. We pass farmhouses near the road. People sit on their porches, rocking. Middle-aged people. Rocking. Some of them wave when we pass.

Jack is gentle and generous, rock solid in his convictions. He's funny and handsome and crazy about me. He's a real catch. And he will not rock on the porch and watch cars and life go by.

I crawl across the seat to his side of the pickup and begin laughing. Ma-niacally. I am laughing so hard I am crying. But I can see through water. ◆

Frank Jamison

CHICAGO IN QUITO
March 9, 2002

Old friend, down from Chicago telling us stories
with grand embellishments, running past midnight,
and of course we love them because after all we are
the characters. This one is of coming from Machu Pichu
and walking the streets of Quito with life everywhere
and pressing and how two soldiers slouch in a doorway
with bandoleers and automatic rifles slung on their shoulders
and he glances their way and sees them stare
with no whites in their eyes, so he looks away and passes
quickly toward the corner and waits to cross over
as a young couple in love comes toward him,
laughing and clumsily bumping him and both apologize
as he recovers nicely in Spanish, proud of being able to do it
and how they are suddenly gone and so is his wallet and pride,
him left there alone with only his bit of Spanish
and the soldiers staring and us here in Tennessee
drinking beer through the night, laughing.

DIAMOND HEAD SUNSET
by Jo Angela Edwins

Jack Rentfro

UNDER A BLUE BIMINI: KEY LARGO

"Biscayne Bay where the Cuban gentlemen sleep all day"—Steely Dan

*B*aby barracuda swim laps between beer cans tossed into Blackwater Bay between sets by the cover band playing its trite boogie at the biker bar.

❧

NOW I'M THE BEER-ACUDA: dreaming of the beer can or the beer can dreaming of the whitest man in Key Largo trying to sunscreen the elemental burn of truth while a lonely Nixon begs someone to talk to him on his ship-to-shore radio. He swears he's not lying anymore. Bebe Rebozo and Bob Ablanalp have left him for someone else. Key lime pie and Cuban coffee all day make you kind of forget what it might have been like if the Santa Maria never sailed this way.

❧

MY ENTIRE REPUTATION seems to rest upon the hinges of the pump in the marine head of a 40-foot sailboat named *Orca*.

❧

TODAY, WE GO SNORKELING for love off the Grecian Rocks or Molasses Point, wherever it isn't too rough. We're going to moon the sunfish and snap back at the snapper and try not to get reefer madness from the reef fish that carry ciguatera wherein toxins build up through each succession in the food chain. Sleeping badly every night—I can hear everything that moves for miles around once the harbor settles down—even conversations in cabins miles away, it seems, plus all the boat sounds in the sound and every morning begins with a harbinger of my own work: the rat-in-a-cage clatter of the laptop keyboard where our hostess works all night so she can party during the day.

✥

LEARNING THE ROPES in the horse latitudes of zero tolerance.

✥

THE NIGHT LOLLING against the bulkhead with the lapping tide until the sun suddenly jumps up and daylight hits you full in the face from the zero degree horizon, making you feel like you've already slept until noon and you still can't evade job anxiety dreams and worrying about things back home as reflected in the weird montage (six days at sea sleeping at four different anchorages never got the city completely out of me, at least, not until I wasn't ready to stay, and my 75 percent rest quotient rendered by my level of sleeping calls for 10 hours to have a good night's rest) and every passing boat in the night becomes a Japanese battleship bearing down on the yacht like it was *PT-109*.

✥

I HEAR THE CENTERBOARD bounce and grate along the silty bottom. On the sixth day out, I was keelhauled and eaten.

✥

I SAW QUITE A FEW turd-brown nurse sharks in the shallows off Rodriguez Key; chasing them down in the rubber Zodiac just like rednecks at a petting zoo, we damn near impaled the dinghy on a scuttled kitchen sink lying upside down, broken pipes breaking the surface like cast iron reeds.

✥

YEAH, THIS CREW IS getting the look of people prepared to travel around the world. Just give me a minute to wipe up the sticky brown rum I spilled that is now snaking rapidly in three directions across the foredeck.

〜◎〜

I AM BECOMING QUITE THE JUDGE of pelican diving teams with their individual styles. At one end of the scale are the ones that simply stop flying and fall into the bay like dead weight. Then, there are the others, the athletes and artists of this sky who water sumo dance. These pelicans pause in mid-air, aerodynamically contour their bodies and enter a downward spiral, hitting the water with a rifling spin.

〜◎〜

OTHER PLAYERS: rich Cubo-Miamians out playing for the day with their pampered children; characters like "Sonny Boy," who hails from Cleveland, Ohio, according to the bouncy script at the stern of his cabin cruiser the size of a troopship who anchors right beside us, refuses to answer radio calls and stays inside with windows closed and generators running all night to enjoy air conditioning; the Coast Guard with its distinctive red diagonal hashmarks on hull; Bluebeard Marine Salvage and Towing; all the "dickheads" as our host-captain refers to the Ocean Reef residents who don't feel obliged to pay attention to the No Wake signs because they *live* here in this seaside millionaires' village; gambling boats heading out of Miami for the territorial limit, party boats also known as Vomit Comets for their astronomic partying.

〜◎〜

WE WATCHED the tropical sunset, anticipating the green flash effect as the sun plops down on the horizon with a great hissing noise amid huge clouds of steam, and we realize that it is simply the backflash of the bikers' cheap Polaroids and land cameras as they take washed-out photographs of the Caribbean Club's waitresses' tits.

〜◎〜

SHORE BIRDS PIPE THE PIPES of Pan in counterpoint to the yelping of rich fishermen chasing baitfish across the bay. One of them, I am pretty sure, is a bottom-feeder.

❧

LAST DAY OF THE VACATION like the last day of summer. I mean: imbued with heavy nostalgia, golden light hueing the end of the fun time and making you keenly aware of the fact that you never really got started having your vacation but just sort of experienced it by default and tomorrow you'll be back home but you want to be back home anyway and you don't know what to say to your hosts whose work has made the visit in stoptime on the treadmill and do you want to be back home to the normal distractions so you won't have so much time to think?

❧

"A YACHT IS any boat you can sleep on," the male host tells us, finally answering the vexatious question plaguing us all through this vacation: just when is a boat a yacht?

❧

sleeping sleeping hearing everything
playing our melodicas for the indifferent tycoon
when his ship comes in
staring back at dusk in the lights of his stateroom
sipping a drink with one of several people who would be glad to
make another for him
as we hoot and holler
from the open cockpit
under a blue bimini

Kristin Robertson

FOLDING THE CRANES

Her hand a hummingbird, an elderly Asian woman
quickly folds my shiny gum wrapper into a small triangle.

I have stopped in the rain at this store in Chinatown,
reflections of a blinking marquee count perfect
seconds across the filmy window,
where live crabs sway and flip in milky water,
round-faced boys hock a thousand sex positions for a dollar.

Four-eighty-two, she whispers, leaning toward me, as if for a secret.

She nods to the cardboard box propping the door
on which a sign reads: *no buy, no change*.
Inside the box I find wings and necks and feet
from greasy paper doilies, sea foam guest checks.

I presume she folds all day, counting to a number that will
save her father from a cancer, lift her sister from a well.
On a train from here, I'll never know, in Wilmington by midnight,
with heat and light, rolls in sweet butter, stars I can see.

Her voice whirls inside me, echoes
pretty bird, luck silver.

Marilyn Kallet

SURVIVOR

The Night of Broken Glass,
thugs set fire to the Rexingen synagogue.
Scorched the *Torah*.
Officials blamed "outsiders."
Or kindergarteners playing with matches.
Jews on the fire brigade who doused the flames
were taken to Dachau

Beginning of the end of three centuries
of Jewish life in Rexingen, Mühringen, Horb.
Sixty emigrated.
Ten "died on the spot."
Others were doomed to Theresienstadt,
Auschwitz, Riga.
After 1942, only one of the Schwarzes
from Horb survived deportation.

Hedwig had seen too much.
She died in Marienhospital, Stuttgart, 1952,
fifty miles from her birthplace.
What held her to the land
of shards and ashes?

Was she lured by the
old cemetery, resting place
of her parents and grandparents?
Was the call of the dead more powerful

than *Shavei Zion*?
Perhaps the leaning firs
of the Black Forest reminded her
of her girlhood, her mother.

Nothing romantic about Terezín.
The ghetto taught her to decipher
tales of witches, children lured
to ovens. A few prisoners
had returned from Auschwitz,
told the truth about "the East."
No gingerbread houses.

But the Red Cross believed
in fairy tales.
For them, Theresienstadt
was a spa, overflowing with Brundibár,
soccer matches, cheerful kids.
After the official visits,
the children were transported to
Auschwitz–Birkenau.
Who could blame the world
for not knowing?

The health care and retirement
package the Nazis had promised
turned out to be typhus, spotted fever,
starvation.

On Sunday, in hospital,
the Sisters of Saint Vincent de Paul
might have wheeled her out for a stroll.
Silence was good medicine,
they thought.

No words to ward off nightfall.
The dead were never far.

Marilyn Kallet

HEDWIG'S STORY
details from "Rexingen Begleiter fur Friedhof und Synagoge"

Dear Great Aunt,
this fragment
reveals only that you
and your husband Louis,
along with the last elderly Jews from
Rexingen, were being transported,
that you "were unable to walk"
and "fell off the car."
Louis tried to help you but they
restrained him August 19, 1942.

I can picture Louis more clearly than
the rest, frantic,
the train pulling away
as you lay helpless.
That hour finished him, though
he didn't die until Theresienstadt.

Some went willingly, we're told.
Nazis had promised "resettlement"
to an "old age home."
At forty-five, you too found the way
to Theresienstadt.
You were "physically challenged."
Crippled.

Forced to stand for hours.
Did the train lurch through the back country
of Rexingen, past the lovely Neckar,
off the known world?

Outside of Prague, past slag heaps,
to Bohušovice station.
From there, prisoners had to march
three miles to Terezín.
But you couldn't walk.
Who carried you to the ghetto?

Hedwig, how did you survive?
The Martyrs Remembrance society
lists you in the camp, 1945,
Liberation.

Then the sisters of Marienhospital
in Stuttgart "cared for"
and "tended to you."
Were you a martyr,
or an ailing woman
who had finally found German mercy?
War's end left three Jews
from Rexingen.
126 had been deported. You alone
returned to Stuttgart, "nearly blind."
You wanted to be buried
in the old Jewish cemetery,
near your mother.
This spring I placed a stone
of remembrance on your grave.

Rest, dear soul.
You survived.
Nearly blind,
you bore witness.

Under the
Jackson Street Bridge 2
by David Habercom

Stones' Throws

Debra X. Poole

RIVER TIME

This southbound mountain stream
blurs my coral toenails,
pushes its shoulder against my calves.

I know its journey.
The frigid stream will split,
one fork cooling spring houses
visited only by ghosts
searching for a drink of buttermilk.
The other fork swooshing through the tourist town,
four fresh lanes of asphalt.

The halves will meet again,
pouring around the joggers' path,
roaring out of the limestone monument—
Scots Irish lost in a burned-out fort.

Dropping into coddling warmer gallons,
spring water merges French Broad and Holston into proud Tennessee.
Muddy home to catfish now,
where coal-laden barges plow the wake
of flat-bottom boats Fort Nashborough bound.

Chief Doublehead paces the soggy bank,
Cherokee warrior mapping bloody miles—
Tuscaloosa
Nashville

Knoxville,
fighting the white tide.

Meandering over the rough bark of gator backs
tired river stretches out,
offers up moody copperheads,
twirls under canoes rocked by giggling girls.
A final burst,
the Gulf of Mexico,
its hard gray pebbles refined by travel
into sugary beach sand.

This mountain water turning my toes blue
goes to glory every minute.
Will rain down on my head come Tuesday.

Steve Sparks

ALONG THE FRENCH BROAD

Always I return to water,
mussel shells in my pocket,
gull feathers to my lips.

A search for something
woven in the cattails and reeds,
or thrown on bank grass to dry.

Silhouetted herons and egrets
are strokes of Buson's pen
along the shoreline,

rotted knots of
cedars and alders
belched onto the beach,

conjure a summer me,
a child on a lake,
running wildly,

slipping off a slick dock
into too shallow water.
My head smacked the
mud bottom, soft
as bedtime kisses,
water warm as spit.

And for a moment I could breathe.

Cold hands yanked me
to the pier where I
flopped and gasped,

a stunned carp,
pulled from one world,
flung into another.

O, rippled water,
lapping at my ankles
like a kicked dog,

no definition of your own,
the color of whatever
looms over you.

Today I am lost, finding
only a cawing crow
feasting on some bloated

thing washed ashore.

Debra A. Poole

BENEATH KENTUCKY LAKE

Crops have gone to brick and stucco,
cows are Wal-Marts now.
Spurning six generations
my cousins and I
abandoned Kentucky
to perch on trendy soil,
scattered from Dallas to Richmond
like acorns by a squirrel.

Our family lands,
scars of tobacco crops,
mule prints,
gardens ripe with mushmellon, okra, and sweet corn,
lie buried under water now,
a weekend skier's highway.

When air was new
Daniel Boone
planted adventurous feet
on grassy Kaintuck ridges,
spied Lookout Mountain two hundred miles south.

On crisp, leaf-crunching days
my children are granted nine miles.
Not far enough to see their kin,
or their roots
sunk deep
at the bottom of the lake.

GRASSROOTS

Drew, 1973

$\mathcal{I}$ don't remember who it was that took the picture, but it wasn't any of my law-abiding neighbors because in 1969, in Lexington, Kentucky, the centerpiece of that photograph was as illegal as sin, not to mention that my blue-blooded mother was in it, grinning like she'd just won a skeet shooting contest. I'm there, too, standing beside her, her arm cinching my waist so that whoever is holding the camera can get us all in.

Clustered on either side are my mother's new friends. They belong to the Blue Springs Country Club, where my father and I play doubles, but that is not where she met them. I know this for a fact because my mother refuses to use the club.

"It's nothing but a white trash place for the new money in town," she told my father when he joined. "And bigots. They don't have black member one."

"Maybe you could encourage the board to change that if you mingled a little," he said.

She lifted her chin and puffed air from her nose, a gesture that said his suggestion was too stupid to entertain. "It's your money," she said. "I suppose you can throw it away if you want."

The fact is that my mother has always been shy among strangers, and had her own pool, which was every bit as nice as the one at the club. The pool was where she and her friends hung out every summer. But for all the yoga and swimming they did, their bottoms sagged below their Catalina swim suits like rag rugs kicked off the floor. These were the women who'd helped my mother sober up, the ones who came to our house the night she finally called AA, the ones who told me how much better life would be for me and my brothers once she'd dried out.

The importance I place on this photograph is, first, that my mother is touching me. It's the only picture in dozens of albums that shows the two of us together. The second is that the reason for my mother's obvious delight, and the thing we're clustered in front of, is a huge marijuana plant I grew in my backyard that summer. It was the only marijuana plant I'd ever grown, and I know now that its enormous size was a chance case of beginner's luck.

The seed that sprouted it came from my California cousin, along with some psychedelic mushrooms I'd stored in the freezer. His instructions were to soak the seed in water until a green sprout broke the husk, but I just tossed it in the ground when I planted the bibb lettuce. My lettuce turned white and tasted bitter. I found out later I should have set it in a shady spot or covered the seedlings with cotton canvas from a tobacco plant bed, but I was a city girl in Capezios and hip-hugger jeans who listened to a lot of Carol King that year. I had the vague notion I could save both myself and my marriage if I heeded her lyrics and "got back to the garden." Vegetables would anchor me to the earth, that was the idea, but my pole beans and Rutgers tomatoes weren't rooting me to anything. They weren't even in that picture. It was the plant that towered above us—like the Norway spruce our local historical society has shipped in from Canada to decorate the Henry Clay home at Christmas. It takes four men to wrestle that tree through the library doors and hoist it up. The marijuana plant would have taken at least that many.

Except for the night my daughter was born, I don't ever remember seeing my mother so enthusiastic about anything. The fact that I had grown the plant in a sedate Chevy Chase suburb, shielded by nothing more than my neighbor's grape arbor and a tall privet hedge on the side facing our house, made it, in her eyes, even more of an event. For the briefest of moments I thought she was pleased by my acquisition of horticulture skills, but the thing that thrilled and excited her was the opportunity to be a renegade, even if it was only by association with me she could get it.

The insight into my mother hit me like a bucket of rocks. This was a woman who had longed to defy tradition and was so fearful of the risks and uncertainties involved she'd stayed to the ruts. That intention must have eaten at her like a cancer every time she made a safe decision. It must have been why she'd been in some stage of drunkenness the whole length of my growing up. She hadn't wanted to get married and have kids and was too scared not to.

If local notoriety was any kind of indicator, I started being outrageous to win her approval at a much earlier age. By the time I entered college, I'd established a pattern of flaunting rules and bearing the terrible consequences of my defiance. Maybe I'd unconsciously sorted these things out when I stuck that seed in the ground. I wonder if I understood the gift I would deliver my mother, a heightened moment of being naughty, the thrill of being a rebel.

Maybe that was why I diligently watered the plant, why I hauled manure home from the racetrack in the boot of my Karmin Ghia. Eventually, redeeming myself by being bad would become the reason I chose dangerously wrong men, dangerously wrong everything. But I'm getting ahead of myself.

❧

IN 1969 THE AROMA from a smoking joint could get you busted in Lexington. We had a newly conceived narcotics squad that was always raiding the only head shop in town, a dark little cavern of a store in a block of downtown marked for urban renewal, where the strongest things sold were incense and patchouli oil. The squad of plain-clothes cops who regularly shook the place down were the same ones who showed up at demonstrations sporting T-shirts emblazoned with peace symbols, reeking of musk and sandalwood and patchouli.

The back yard where my garden was located was long and narrow; from the house the lot sloped to a street which dead-ended in rolling pasture and the university's aboretum. Except for neighbors, there was little traffic. I hadn't given much thought to the pot plant's size until it began shading my bountiful zucchini crop, and one afternoon I got out the hedge shears and mercilessly pruned the branches. I didn't know this would make it grow even fuller.

Zucchini might just be my favorite vegetable, and that first year of gardening I grew them so big I had to borrow a hand saw to slice them.

I set planks between two sawhorses and cut the squash into manageable pieces before taking them in the house. For a first grade history project, my daughter selected a zucchini the size of a country ham and we hollowed it out, canoe fashion, and painted it to resemble birch bark. The kids were studying Lewis and Clark, and my daughter patiently explained her project's relevance to me—how friendly Indians had helped the party make canoes that would take them to the Pacific Ocean. "They really used trees, Mom," she said as we applied the final coat of lacquer. On parents' night, the last day of school, with the Lewis and Clark projects ranged around the room, I learned, indirectly, that a fastidious gardener gathers her zucchini when they're small and tender.

My success with squash led to thoughts of renting country acreage the next spring and organizing a farmers' market to make my vegetables pay, but I discovered supply and demand working against me. Every garden in town produced its bounty when mine did. These were not exactly idle thoughts. If Ben and I separated, I would need an income. Briefly, I toyed with the idea of selling the plant. At rallies and demonstrations, I'd met dozens of gardeners who didn't grow marijuana.

Because of my indifferent pruning, the plant was topping out at twenty-six feet, fourteen across at the base. It dominated my garden. Only patchy sunlight reached the ground. My pole beans turned white, the zucchini quit growing, and my husband, who traveled during the week, became aware of a peculiarly sweet odor one Friday when he pulled into the garage. "It's the garden," I said. "I'm growing herbs."

One afternoon, I crossed the street to see if the plant showed above the roof line of our green-shuttered cottage. I stood on the opposite sidewalk and strained to see over the sweet gum tree and climbing hydrangea that grew on the side of the house away from the drive. No, I decided, the sight line wasn't going to be the problem in keeping my plant a secret until harvest, whenever that was. The smell would give me away. I could inhale its seductive aroma all over the neighborhood. I thought about the garbage men and paper boys, the kids pushing lawnmowers up and down the street all summer. I wondered if they knew.

THE SECOND TIME I saw my mother's new friends, a week after her phone call for help, they were sitting around the coffee table in a hospital lounge. The air conditioning was turned so high the windows were fogged. Every muscle in my body drew up in the cold. My head throbbed painfully. "Your father's with her doctor," Anna Jane said as I slid into a seat. I was in tennis shorts, sweating so hard my thighs sealed themselves to the green vinyl.

I glanced at my watch. Thirty minutes earlier, I'd answered a telephone page at the tennis court. I should get to the hospital immediately. "ER," the voice had said.

My bare skin felt clammy on the chrome arm rests, and I leaned forward, propping my elbows on my knees, clinching my hands as if chronic worry could somehow help my mother.

Marguerite reached over and patted my knee. "She's going to make it," she said.

Across the table, Anna Jane Sterling twisted a Camel into a cigarette holder and dug in her purse for the propane lighter she carried. She was short and stout with gold and silver streaked hair and wine red fingernails. When we met, she'd told me how, by giving up gin and tonic, she'd outlived three husbands and inherited their fortunes. Anna Jane snapped the lighter and a blue flame hissed. She inhaled deeply and leaned against the side cushions on the couch, recrossing her legs in preparation to speak. The other women, Renee and Marguerite, had husbands who took my father to Alanon meetings when he was in town. They waited to let Anna Jane say her piece first.

My mother's friends struck me as worldly and sophisticated, although, as I got to know them, I discovered they were each first generation off the farm. My mother was too, her first move being when she was sent from the bottomland farm at Owens Branch to a girls' school in Tennessee. Sometime after that, my grandfather moved his coal business to Lexington and bought a house on fashionable Bell Court. If there were ever any hayseeds in my mother's hair, she shook them out there.

Anna Jane gazed at me through a stream of blue smoke. "It'll take thirty days to get the booze out, Drew, honey," she said. "Don't expect much. Your mama's about to pass through a new kind of hell."

"Not a pretty sight," Marguerite said. They exchanged knowing looks. Renee pursed her red lips and breathed over a Dixie cup of hot coffee. "She won't be easy to live with when she gets home," she said.

"I wouldn't have any friends over if I were you," Marguerite added.

Anna Jane flicked her cigarette toward a full ashtray. "What we're saying, darlin', is that you shouldn't expect her *behavior* to improve for a while. Knowing how pig-headed your mama is, she'll take her own sweet time."

I wanted to ask them if my mother would like me any better when she was sober, but I was afraid to. I didn't want them to know how important it was. I made a pact with myself. I would do whatever it took to help her get well. Eventually, she'd come around and realize what a good daughter I was. I know how crazy this sounds, but when I was sixteen I lived and breathed in my mother's shadow. My essence was garnered from the day-to-day reflections of myself I saw in her pale blue eyes. I wasn't exactly without self-esteem. I was without identity.

All this happened eight years before the photograph in my garden was taken, and although my mother had remained sober since the day a neighbor found her on the bathroom floor, unconscious and near death, her bloody wrists sliced near to the bone, I can't honestly say that her recovery changed our relationship for the better. I'm immensely grateful she's alive. I really am. But just because she joined AA and took up yoga and reading Thomas Merton didn't make my life any easier. I can't speak for my brothers. I see the two that aren't completely psychotic from time to time, and they've more or less survived our family, but they're not exactly happy people.

❦

WHEN THE SHUTTER SNAPPED, my mother and her friends were giggling like college girls at a bootlegger's. Quickly, my mother removed her hand from my waist and snipped some leaves off the plant with a pair of fingernail scissors she pulled from her purse. She presented a cluster of leaves to each of the women, then popped several in her mouth and began to chew. "What happens now?" she said in a bright voice.

"I don't know," I said. "Nothing," would have been the honest answer, not even if it was hashish. But I didn't say this. It was too pleasant seeing her show off for her friends, watching her retie a pretty Mexican sarong over her bathing suit and pretend to be bad. The other women swallowed their leaves and stuck out their tongues to see whose was greenest. They talked like they'd grown up someplace else. They all had voices that sounded like whiskey.

They had left their bridge game by the pool and come to take my daughter for ice cream, but she had napped through their visit. She was still sleeping when they passed through the privet hedge and strolled back to my mother's station wagon. "We'll take Charlotte for ice cream tomorrow, if it suits you," my mother said. She was walking in front of me and stopped so abruptly I almost ran into her. "Judas Priest," she said in a husky whisper. "Maybe someone will see it." She paused to consider the possibilities. "I wonder if they'll call the police," she said after a moment. Her eyes narrowed and she looked at me so shrewdly I thought she could see all the reasons I had for letting the marijuana plant grow, the reasons I had before I'd ever thought of selling it.

I wanted to wrap my arms around her and tell her that I loved her until she heard me, to tell her she should do whatever made her happy, and if that included eating pot or skating on the thin edge of the law, it was okay with me. I wanted to tell her that I'd accepted her bad genes for alcohol with gratitude because they were part of the package, that I needed her still, that I wouldn't have wanted anyone else for my mother. I don't know why I couldn't say this, but that's the way it was.

"You could be arrested for that plant," she said, her voice rising as she drew out the word "arrested." "My daughter the outlaw," she said. She smiled and touched my cheek.

"I'll cut it down," I said. "It's going to kill my vegetables if I don't do something."

"I wouldn't go that far," she said, opening the station wagon door. She eased down on the leather seat and laid a freckled arm on the door. "Is that what smells?" she asked pleasantly.

I nodded.

Her friends climbed in and she started the engine and backed into the street before I could get past the confusion of her hand on my cheek. I'd made a pitcher of iced tea and had planned to invite them in, but because my daughter was sleeping they had wandered into the back-yard and discovered the plant. I wanted their visit to be more average, more a normal mother visiting her daughter and granddaughter, more of something I knew existed and couldn't put my finger on. But she had wanted her picture taken with the marijuana plant to feel like she was breaking the rules that had made her drink and then, after she got sober, made her mean.

The women in the station wagon raised their Coppertone arms and waved back at me, sunlight winking off their bangle bracelets. "Bye-bye," they called.

"Come back," I said. I waited, watching her back out and shift into drive and pull away. The car was almost out of sight when I began a conversation with her. "By the way," I said, "that plant won't get any taller. It's got just so much time for growing. A season. It flourished because I gave it everything it needed, sun and food and water—and love. Plants are a lot like us, except we've got longer seasons."

My mother tooted the horn when she turned the corner. I swear, she knew I was talking to her and wanted me to know she wasn't listening. I thought I might as well get it all off my chest. I walked down the driveway and opened the gate in the picket fence. "Listen," I said. "I'll grant you that's a fine pot plant, but what about my novel, the one displayed on your coffee table making some kind of statement about how supportive you've been? The one you told your buddies you had no intention of reading. I guess you're waiting for me to make something of myself before going to the trouble. Well, I have made something of myself. You just didn't notice."

I moved into the house and stood in the kitchen with the refrigerator open. I fanned myself with the cold air until my heart stopped pounding and my skin cooled. In the next room I heard my daughter stir in her sleep. It was time for her to get up. My stomach clenched when it occurred to me how pleased my mother would be if I got busted for cultivating a marijuana plant. So simple. If I got busted my mother could be wild by association, bad without taking chances—and she would keep my beloved daughter until I got out of jail. It is more than a little conceivable that this is what had prompted that generous smile when her fingers brushed my cheek.

I sat down on the side of my little girl's bed and watched her come awake. Pretty soon I would take her in my arms and tell her how it would be as she grew up and grew away from me, how it would never be like it was for me and my mother. I wanted her to know I would pass to her a clean legacy of love, that I would never deny or manipulate her or shame her in any way for something I should had done differently with my life. I would encourage her to be happy, to hold to that value of happiness, and that from this moment on I would set her an example to follow, and when I could not do that,

I would point her in the direction of better choices than I had made. But the truth of things was that my daughter loved her grandmother. The truth was that my mother bought my child's love in ways too subtle to articulate, too subtle for a little girl to understand, and I would only alienate them both if I told the truth.

⟜⊙⟞

THAT NIGHT I tossed and turned in the double bed until Ben turned on the light. He rolled over and propped himself up on an elbow. "What's going on?" he said. "Why can't you sleep?"

"Do you think it's going to rain?" I asked.

"How the hell should I know? You're the farmer."

"I think I should turn the sprinkler on my garden," I said. "The squash leaves looked wilted."

"I think I need to get to sleep," he said. He rolled away from me and switched off the light. "Don't lie there and breathe like that, Drew. It drives me crazy."

I climbed out of bed, found my jeans and dressed in the dark. Ben was breathing steady as the tides when I closed the bedroom door. The moon was nearly full and I had no problem finding the tools I wanted in the shed. I took down the regulation Boy Scout hatchet from its place on the pegboard. I found my file. I sat on a lawn chair under our gingko tree, the moon catching silver in my hands every time I drew the file over the blade of the hatchet. When the steel was honed to my satisfaction I stepped through the hedge and began chopping. Golden half moons of woody stalk scattered at my feet. About half-an-hour later I stepped back, dripping sweat, my arms sticky with resin. The plant swayed drunkenly, toppled and crashed to the ground. Methodically, I hacked off the limbs and chopped them into aromatic chunks. When that was done, I hefted the pitchfork and proceeded to turn what may have been the biggest marijuana plant in all Kentucky into the compost heap. Tomorrow the sun would shine and the heat begin its work. ◆

117

Sara Small

THE BOTANIST AND HIS WIFE

can't take a walk around the block
without a game of identification: He points.
>She: Maple.
>He: Yes, but which kind?
>She (shrugging): Sugar? Red?
>He (sighing): *Acer saccharinum.* Silver maple. See
>>how the bark peels and how the lobes of the leaves
>>are jagged and deep?
>She (sidestepping): Watch out for the dogsh—. Nevermind.

Back home he kills plants. First day of spring,
he sends the philodendron and African violet out
to sun on the porch, imagining their chloroplastic ecstasy.
Instead their leaves are scorched, crisp
as potato chips around the edges.
>She: Stay away from my plants. Don't dip
>>Your fingers in my flower beds.
>He (head hanging): Well, I just thought—
>She (arms akimbo): And don't go near the garden, either.

(where he pulls the stems off of onions, picks cucumbers
before the prickers have softened, and lets zucchini grow
monstrous like some forbidden radioactive experiment)

FIRST KISS
by Ellen Agee

Patricia Wellingham-Jones

First Time Around the Block Alone

The child nods her head solemnly,
lump of brown hair bouncing
under a red barrette. Takes her baby sister
by the reluctant hand. The list of "don'ts"
rings in her ears. She starts down
the sidewalk at Grandmother's house,
feeling very big in her five-year-old's shoes.
On the porch the family elders wave and smile.

The girls march to the corner, turn right.
Big sister slants her eyes at the grownups
still watching. Little sister mutters,
tugs her hand loose. The big one
grabs a bit harder, hisses instructions.

At the corner the adventure goes astray.
The big one turns right, responsible child that she is;
the little one yanks her hand free, darts to the street.
Across a road empty of traffic and up the sidewalk
she scampers, yelling over her shoulder, "No, no, no!"

Because she was told to go straight around the block
big sister plods the long way home.
She appears from the right place,
wrong number of children.

First Time Around the Block Alone

Adult screams fill the air on the porch.
Tears rain, sobs choke, hands wring
and she wets her pants as she gasps out the story
of what went wrong. Grownups fly from the house
in all directions.

Four blocks away the little one
rocks on a verandah,
sips lemonade, nibbles her third brownie.
Gives her hostess a chocolaty smile.
Enchanted, the woman blinks
when a man rushes to her doorstep,
scoops up the child with a shout of relief.

Big sister sobs in her sleep for a week,
little one dreams of candy.

Susanna Greenberg

Co-Pilots

$\mathcal{S}$outhern Virginia isn't hiding much. Seems to like its waitresses' tops tight and its elementary schools pristine. Exhausted by a neon hotel lobby after midnight, we take the one-bed Arabian themed room, just to make a splash in this unforgiving town. North Carolina seems to sway between her inner North and her inner Carolina. The humid picnic tables of Bubba's BBQ sit across the way from a store selling all things hemp and goddess-friendly. A roadside church reads, *"If God is your co-pilot, switch seats."* But in the field where the Wright Brothers' first plane took twelve baby steps, we learn that while Wilbur flew it, Orville ran alongside, holding its wing steady, and this partnership appeals to us more. Their risky venture is now etched in Carolina stone in words that become our anthem of sorts for this journey: *Conceived in genius, achieved by dauntless resolution and inconquerable faith.*

We refuse to feel herded. Nothing can go wrong when you have no plan, we announce gleefully to the road before us, daring it to try to shape our journey's angles and curves into a sensible polygon. "Way" will be a loose word for us, we declare, so nothing is out of our way. The story will be told in the receipts, from gas stations without debit swipes, late-night Dairy Queens and outlet stores shamefully chosen over the Smoky Mountains and their Dolly Parton theme park.

Through wrought-iron gates in Charleston, South Carolina, we sneak peeks into courtyards in which sweet tea and books could well approximate heaven. We agree to retire here, guilt-free, when the world is saved enough for our tastes. The marshes of the National Wildlife

Refuge outside this lovely town make us envy its native species. The government is doing well by these birds and lizards, who know where they belong.

Savannah is shy, hiding in well-planned squares behind Spanish moss that obscures the view from invasive northern eyes that think they understand cities. We choose roads by landscape, and so choose which disclosures to hear. Georgia surely has other stories, but knowing we can't do it justice with a whisper-down-the-lane drive-through wave, we stick to its highways. Interstates are good for picking apart men we have known, while arrow straight roads through farmland draw endless musing on urban realities. And on twisting forest roads at midnight, we sink into our deepest worries of what work we are alive to do and whether we can do it.

Tennessee tries to divert us to tourist tracks. Though the root beer float was good, and the guy on the corner did look like Willie Nelson, the side streets of Knoxville give away Nashville's secret—white folks can be mighty poor too.

Outside each town, the rings of franchise tighten like choke collars. We jump through the hoops, learning that the cheap hotel ring will always fall between car dealerships and mid-range chain restaurants. (Do not say sprawl has no method to its madness.)

When every state reveals that it too bought the big box super store kit and unpacked it right here on our road, we bemoan the commodified landscape, with mandatory angst that feels as clichéd as the strips themselves.

And when we find those unpolluted roads that don't force our eyes to edit billboards out of mountain faces, we get uneasy, worried that we've gone where we do not belong. This is why Kentucky disturbs us, spookily foreign. Where any two houses lie close enough to be called neighbors, a road sign always warns "Congested area. 35 miles per hour." We try to leave our expectations of refrigeration and dental care at the state line but cannot and find ourselves cruel. Finally, a McDonald's emerges from the flat landscape. But The Ten Commandments are hanging on the wall, weighing judgment on us, and we have a long drive still ahead, without bad directions from the manager.

Thankfully we are released into West Virginia, which defies our low expectations by letting our hearts out on its deep green hills. I didn't know how clouds could light up after sunset until now. These police-men are no match for our charms. By the third time we are stopped, we plead for directions in a perfect mirroring of his uniformed drawl. Our one hundred mile per hour blaze is entirely forgivable, once again, as we subject him to unrelenting smiles.

Pennsylvania, which gave birth to us, returns us safely to our urban den, and we take its scenic route. There is ownership here. We know the guy on the welcome sign; we answered the phones that put him there. It is only appropriate to watch fireworks in the distance, on the 4th of July, as we see our state whole, ourselves whole, and return to familiar roads. ◆

Christine Parkhurst

WAITIN' ON THE SUNSET

Waitin' on the Sunset

Just killing a few hours at the zoo.
Ambling slow.
Dripping sweat.

Big Cottonmouth hissed through the glass.
Came right up and gave two split tongue lashes.
Whippitgood, whippitgood.

Whoa, that's enough abuse, Jack, and
I'm out of this reptile house in a flash.

Back in the sun.
Too hot.

Should have gone shopping instead.
It's such a man's world.

Laura Still

NIGHT BIKING
for Maureen

The dark can be your friend—if you're not afraid,
and you learn how to use it
she said, invisible except
for white stripes in her sweater.
She invited me to go night biking at Kiawah
one early October night before moonrise
when icy sparks of brilliance
hung the heavens, almost clustered close
enough to hear their faraway frozen music,
the Milky Way trailing frosty smoke
across the firmament.

I'd spent too many years in the sun,
white hard light that blackens skin
bleaches bone, never flinches,
dries everything—
    rain, fruit, blood.
Night was for sleep
pulling me deep in its undertow,
only to find a thirst even drowning
couldn't quench.

So I've pedaled after her
down many a tree-crowded lane
counting their low hung branches,

Night Biking

bumps from uneven pavement, or
yellow eyes of ocelots in underbrush
as reasonable risks.
I've slipped into darkness like a skin,
    learned to see
light collected in grains of silica
glowing up from the path,
    guided my wheel
through hazards of tree roots
or soft mould, slippery with decay.

We've cruised alligator holes,
splashed through sprinklers,
climbed spiral stairs of a bird tower
to watch stars mirrored in marsh pools.
A brassy corona on the horizon
warned us to pedal madly towards the strand,
to see the full moon born
in a pool of molten gold
spreading on the sea.

Missed turns, mosquito bites, bruises,
    blisters, sore muscles,
    lost sleep
are small change paid
    to discover
I can be good
    in the dark.

RAMSEY CASCADE
by Matt Forsythe

Kim Trevathan

STRADDLING GENRES:
FACT AND FICTION IN THE
TRAVEL NARRATIVE

I'm in a boat, a small one, immersed in damp darkness, big walls rising up all around, the chamber aromatic of slackwater, scum, and dead fish. My dog, Jasper, staggers for balance in the bow of my boat, a canoe. From below comes the roar of water rushing through valves, lowering us to the level of the next reservoir. We should be descending gently as in a giant draining bathtub; instead, we are rushing forward and spinning, like a cork in a tilting, thrashing ocean. Now I'm sitting upright in a bed. To starboard, instead of the dark, scummy walls of a dam's lock, there's the plate glass window of a hotel room. My wife sleeps beside me. To port glares the fluorescent bathroom light. Below me, where the room's thin carpeting should be, the Tennessee River rolls darkly, slyly past—not the modern river, its muscle long eviscerated by nine dams—but the wild, unrestrained version I'd read about in history books, the hotel room bed sluicing the current as if it were one of the boulders the Tennessee Valley Authority had submerged half a century ago. Jasper, on the floor/water, flinches in his own river nightmare.

I was blessed with these nightmares on overnight breaks in my five-week canoe trip down the Tennessee River in 1998, content for my book, *Paddling the Tennessee River: A Voyage on Easy Water*. The dreams, as I say in the book, were a signature of my growing intimacy with the river. It would not leave me alone, even when I left it for the sterilized homogeneity of a hotel room. Continuing for months after the trip ended, the nightmares thrust me into a sort of limbo between the horror and surrealism of bad dream-life and the half-awake perception that steers one through an unfamiliar hotel room in the dark. As such, they fascinated me more than anything else about the trip, and I looked forward to them as to feasts of the imagination. They transcended logic and research and enabled me to get at truths that elude fact-based narrative: that the river transcended the blandness of its modern incarnation, a mute string of lakes, that it had the power not only to invade my dreams but to violate the border between unconscious and waking life, between the present and the past. That the dreams "happened" makes them nonfiction, but their "content" gets at the root of what's best about fiction: what we can create beyond our conscious efforts.

⌐◦⌐

"WHY CAN'T YOU just stay at home and write like normal people?"

This was a question from my well-intentioned wife, Julie, in response to my next planned canoe trip, down the length of the Cumberland River: 696 miles, five dams, a major metropolis (Nashville), a 70-foot waterfall, and an embarkation point known as "Bloody Harlan." Five years had passed since the Tennessee River trip, a half-decade that made its mark on me. I seriously pondered this question. Indeed, why didn't I stay home and write fiction like most of my friends, who felt just fine about making things up or drawing upon the experiences of their youth for inspiration and content? I had published short fiction, and I had written novels, albeit unpublished. Why was I compelled to *do* something, and then write a fact-based account of it? Wouldn't an imagined narrative of a trip down the Cumberland pack more power, more depth, more literariness than another in the long list of paddle narratives that had been written about every river wider than a stone's throw?

To answer this question is to examine my character as a writer at this point in my life. In the late nineties I worked for a dot com company, which in those boom times of exhilaration and bombast provided me with ready-made characters full of color, complexity, and quirkiness; settings absurd enough to make Kafka cringe; and an intense, slow-burning anger stoked with several levels of perceived and actual injustice. After the inevitable layoff at the turn of the century (and even during my employment there), bitter fiction poured out of me. In one, a humiliated salesman stops at a pawn shop on his way to work and tries to buy rubber bullets for his grandfather's .22 pistol; in another, a nightmare of post-layoff guerilla warfare rages through the suburbs among executives, middle management, and "content workers"; another follows a group of employees around San Francisco on a humiliating, skateboard scavenger hunt intended to promote worker morale. Because of the incredulity and anger with which I looked back upon my dot com experiences, fiction writing seemed the best (though not the only) outlet, enabling me to avenge those who had exploited me for five years: tight-lipped middle managers in love with phrases such as "unacceptable performance" and "necessary sacrifice" and "team player," and the aloof, know-nothing executives who had dangled the carrot of a modest stock option payoff that rotted because of their ineptitude, who floated safely across the stormy waters of unemployment on their golden parachutes. I still get worked up about it.

Why not take the experiences of the Tennessee River voyage and turn them into a fictional account of a canoe trip down the Cumberland? I could even use some of the historical research I'd already done on the Cumberland. I could create a main character (a more interesting, heroic version of myself, à la Daniel Day Lewis) who ponders the courage, self absorption, and tragedy of Daniel Boone's life, the drama of the Eastern Kentucky coal mining wars, the wonder of the first white men to see (and tumble over) Cumberland Falls, the despair of one-armed, one-legged General John Bell Hood watching the Confederacy breathe its last at the Battle of Nashville. Perhaps most importantly, why not create *fictional* conflicts (and resolutions) between the main character and the people in cabin cruisers who nearly swamp him, instead of experiencing them firsthand?

For one thing, I like the uncertainty of an actual trip, the gap that inevitably widens between what I expect and what happens. Harlan frightened me because of its violent history, because of the paranoia of the post 9/11 era, and because a man who actually *swam* the length of the Cumberland told me that someone shot at him from a bridge in Harlan County, that he was routinely terrorized at camp sites. On this trip, I would have greater responsibilities. Instead of Jasper in the bow,

Randy Russell, a photographer, would accompany me. As much as I loved Jasper, the possibility that my project might endanger the life of another human raised the stakes. On the ride from Knoxville to Harlan to drop us off, friends Murray Browne and Ian Joyce, both wiseass northerners, cracked *Deliverance* jokes the whole way. Randy and I laughed, though uneasily. What would happen to us? Would one of us get hurt? Go mad? How would our worries pan out? Were we worried about the right things?

In preparation for this trip and the last one I did two kinds of research. historical background and first-hand observation. I'd read about Boone, Andrew Jackson, and Thomas Jefferson's murderous nephews in Smithland, Kentucky, our destination, to prepare myself for the river's potentialities. On the trip, I wanted to find out what remained of the depravity, courage, and resourcefulness of an area's historical precursors. According to Harriet Arnow's *Seedtime on the Cumberland*, James Robertson, one of the early leaders of the settlement that would become Nashville, applied what he'd learned from a French doctor to the victim of a scalping, David Hood; using an awl, he drilled holes through Hood's scull, allowing what oozed out to form a "scablike covering" where the scalp had been. Hood lived 20 more years. A brutal remedy, yes, but also genius: what would remain of this frontier resourcefulness in what we now know as Music City? Not much, as it turned out. Nashville by canoe I cannot recommend, unless Gulliverlike, you want your misanthropy confirmed. After we locked through Old Hickory Dam and floated on strong current toward downtown, a gang of teen toughs hailed us from the bank: "Get out of that canoe!" Not a mile farther we sighted an approaching cabin cruiser towing a houseboat at full throttle on a river 30 yards wide, carving a double wake four feet high. "Welcome to Nashville!" said a shirtless man, toasting us with a beer can, his gut hairy and distended. Most of Randy's camera equipment was soaked in the resulting wake storm. The Nashvillians did not look back. This would be one of many such encounters, and it would jolt me out of my meditations on the vestiges of resourceful pioneer ghosts around Music City.

The first-hand observation before the trip—such as canoeing a few miles up the Caney Fork River, a major Cumberland tributary that snakes under Interstate 40 five times within ten miles of the road—served to familiarize us with segments of the journey so that we could pick out a few camping sites, note a grocery store near the bank, or learn by talking to fisherman how to catch the local trout. I put a halt to both kinds of research before they became exhaustive, before I knew too much. At a recent talk about my Tennessee River book, a woman asked why I didn't motorboat the entire river before I canoed it. I told her that I didn't want to know what was waiting around each bend, that the tension created during the trip, my wondering who or what I might confront and where I would camp for the night, was a tension I desired in the resulting narrative. Though I scouted it beforehand, nothing could have prepared me for the campsite at Sawyer, in Kentucky, about fifteen miles downstream from Cumberland Falls. It was there that Randy awoke me from an afternoon nap and said I had to follow him, that I had to see *this*, though he wouldn't elaborate. I still don't know what it was exactly, though I can say that there had been some outdoor worshipping at one campsite, complete with a stone garden, a framed picture of Jesus, an offering plate, small benches, and crude drawings placed on the picnic table. A purple shirt was draped over an iron hook. It was streaked with something red. No one was about, but the vibes of primitivism sent chills up my spine. The possibility that we might hear folks in the woods speaking in tongues or handling snakes created exquisite fear and dread, no matter that it didn't happen.

Meeting with the unexpected and unplanned wouldn't guarantee that I'd be blessed with the fiction writer's staple of narrative tension: obstacles. That's the quandary of the nonfiction travel narrative. You want the trip itself to go smoothly so that you can enjoy yourself and come back home in sufficient mental and physical health to write up the account, yet you don't want the trip to be so smooth that an account of it is innocuous, like small talk with a stranger:

Day One: beautiful, not too hot, nice breeze.

Day Two: we caught a fish and ate it, met some nice fishermen from the area.

Day Three: we're bored and sunburned and the current is slowing. Damn the barges.

That's part of the trap of any narrative, fictional or factual. Depending upon external conflict sometimes causes writers to miss more provocative internal turmoil: nightmares, what-if scenarios, the influence of the dead. I hoped that my father, who died of cancer soon after the last trip, unable to see the publication of my book, would make an appearance somewhere along the Cumberland and tell me something. He did not cooperate. My mother said he probably approved of this trip, unlike the last, because I had Randy along and didn't go alone. As it turned out, conflicts would arise between Randy and me, subtly, without warning, coming more from my growing resemblance to Captain Ahab and Gulliver than I cared to admit.

I suppose that taking these canoe trips instead of writing fiction might be my version of paying dues, of assuaging some need to suffer for pursuing the writer's life. Yet I have no delusions about my little voyages: they are modest cakewalks compared to what others undertake in far remoter regions covering vast amounts of territory under extreme conditions. I am no adventurer who writes; I'm a writer who uses adventure for research, for material. And I prefer the familiar, the regional to the exotic, though exotica often appear in familiar territory.

❦

DETERMINED TO END my Tennessee River voyage on deadline (I had to return to the dot com job), tired of camping and eating out of cans, I paddled forty-two miles of flat water on the last day, including a lockage through Kentucky Dam. I was on the water seventeen hours, starting out in the dark at 3:00 a.m. and arriving in the dying twilight of Paducah at 8:00 p.m. Wary of monster barges crossing back and forth across the river, skirting an industrialized riverfront stinking with diesel fuel and other chemicals, I paddled hard through the darkness, my mind fixed on one goal: reaching the end where my family waited. Something to port distracted me: a sculpture on the bank, big as a garage, flooded in white light. It was Neptune who stood before me in full glory, with his trident and massive head, the beard flowing down across his wide chest. It seemed an odd place for a sculpture, in the midst of this industry, engines idling, towboats hooting, but then I thought it might be an art foundry and this riverbound Neptune advertised the work of the artists. As I paddled closer, Neptune was transformed into a bush, its shadow cast backward against an industrial elevator. Neptune sounded a keynote for the voyage, a ghost whose significance transcended all the others—Ulysses S. Grant, Nathan Bedford Forrest, Colonel John Donelson—each of whom I had willfully conjured during the voyage and in the resulting book. In making his appearance unbidden, Neptune, with his trident, was showing me the way off the river, telling me it was time to return to my life on the land.

The Cumberland invaded my dreams just as the Tennessee had, in a hotel room near Carthage, the hometown of Al Gore, where Julie and Randy's girlfriend Lara met us. It flowed along the hotel room floor as I sat up and entered that familiar limbo, half in this world, half in the river's grasp. From this, I confirmed that the Cumberland and the Tennessee were part of a sisterhood, pranksters who visited in my weakest, most vulnerable moments, when I thought I had escaped them for a rest. As it turned out, I wouldn't hallucinate on the Cumberland, at least not in the same way I did on the Tennessee, though I witnessed plenty—human, animal, and meteorological—that rivaled the best hallucinations of my life.

In his essay, "A Working Boy's Whitman," George Evans points out the gap between the great poet's imagined travels and his actual wanderings, noting that his poetry suffers because of that gap. The role of the imagination in fabricating events and scenes is obvious; perhaps more subtle is the imagination required to render an actual experience as compelling as what one might read in a novel or poem. While adhering to facts, resisting the tall tale, careful about proportions and details, the nonfiction writer must shape and re-envision. He may have fewer decisions to make about plot, character, and setting, but many options about shaping those elements of experience that require the hard work of the imagination and a consensual trust between reader and writer about fact, nuance, and the reportage of non-factual content, such as personal mythology, nightmares, and other tricks of the mind. ◆

Bill Brown

SPELUNKING

On a trip to see the formation room
in Wolf River Cave, the geologist
said not to worry about claustrophobia,
worry about bumping your head.
Our lights angled the darkness away
as we stooped and turned, twisting
our shoulders through tight crevasses.
Stepping down, stepping up,
our hands monitored where the light
didn't reach. After an hour of close
scrambling and the occasional
echo room caked with guano,
our guide whispered that we must
crawl 200 yards to reach the formations.
He added that the cave was living,
not to alter our surroundings
with movements. Knees, elbows,
and twisting hips, I thought about
being in the colon of a stone beast.
I wondered how my life had come
to this, a cave polyp. I empathized
with Jonah. When I tried to raise
my chest, the guide said you'll chip
a million years off that stalactite.
I felt like Judas, his pockets lined
with silver. I remembered the short
lovely lives of butterflies. I thought

about my brother's epilepsy, how
after seizures, he pieced together
fragments of his immediate past.
I wondered why I avoided therapy.
I thought hard for Stafford's fawn,
and remembered a news article
about a pregnant woman found
dead in a blizzard, her fetus living,
waiting to be born.

Judy Loest

EVE, LEAVING THE GARDEN
FOR GOOD, 1953

In this Appalachian version, Eve came home one day
With a bucket of hard green apples to be cooked
On the coal stove and served over biscuits for breakfast.
Out in the field, she had had a vision, a recollection
Of an ad in *Life Magazine* for an electric stove.
Adam had no choice but to help carry into another state
Her handmade quilts, the winter coats ordered
With egg money from the *Chicago Mail Order Catalog*,
The child's summer dresses sewn from flour sacks.
Never one to eat of the bread of idleness,
In the new land Eve learned to drive, got a job,
Bought school clothes on layaway at J.C. Penney's.
She opened a bank account, taking her own counsel
Like a bright fruit, as if it were her due.

Rising while it was still night, scraping snow and ice
From the windshield in winter, she left lunch money
On the table, hot oatmeal on the G.E. range.
While still a young woman, she buried the sickly Adam
But not before he had learned to praise her.
Her children rose up and called her blessed.
Sometimes, she and her daughter,
Visiting in the summer, would drive back through Eden,
Stopping to buy homemade apple butter and fresh corn.
Eve would recount her life matter-of-factly, like scenes
From a book she had once read, remark how narrow
The roads were, how small everything seemed.

David E. Joyner

The Pilgrimage of
Geoffrey Pinkerton

I don't belong among the diapered
and bibbed droolers who wander aimlessly through the corridors of
Pineview. For starters, I'm not as old as the others. Oh, I may forget
things now and then, and maybe I did get lost, but only once. No reason to incarcerate me with a roommate who can't recall his own name,
who shuffles around in terrycloth slippers because he's forgotten how
to tie his shoes. It is a habitat which would strip me of my sanity were it
not for the garden into which I withdraw; a landscape of the past where
fragments of childhood tease and flash before me so real I can almost
touch them before they slip beyond my grasp. Yet it is a wilting garden,
poorly tended, where my parched mind, like Snow White's mirror, can
no longer be trusted to separate the real from the imagined.

But today is different. It's both my birthday and the dawn of a new millennium. The image of Carrie Spangler that has haunted me all morning lures
me back to my eleventh birthday and the blood vow which Carrie and I put
on paper and tucked behind a loose stone in the retaining wall below my
house at 327 Locust—an address I can't forget because I helped Daddy paint
the numbers on the top riser of its granite steps when I was six. The image is
one that will not leave, one that admonishes me to honor my commitment.

❧

THE SPANGLERS LIVED NEXT DOOR in the largest house in Centerville—a turreted and lavishly ornamented Queen Anne whose dark and
varnished innards smell of wax. Carrie and I huddled against the wall as

we watched the movers. The third moving van backed into the drive under the watchful eye of Mrs. Spangler and maneuvered as closely as it dared to the porte cochère. It took two days to empty the mansion of its contents while Carrie and I marveled at the skill with which the sweating giants lifted sideboards, massive mirrors and even a grand piano into the trucks, all the while having to check their language and abstain from spitting.

Dr. Spangler had accepted a staff position at Johns Hopkins. The family would leave the next day. Lengthening afternoon shadows stretched across the lawn and up the steps as if to blanket the past, to tuck it back into yesterday with a farewell prayer. And why did it have to be on my birthday that Carrie and I had to face maybe never seeing each other again?

Carrie culled a penny that was minted on the year of my birth from her coin collection. She polished it, wrapped it in a scented handkerchief, and placed it in the pocket of a card she made from her father's letterhead, which she folded and pasted together with flour and water. The card contained the words, in her small cursive hand, of a vow composed that morning:

"We, Geoffrey Pinkerton and Carrie Spangler, being of sound mind and body, promise to meet at sunset on this date in the year of our Lord, two-thousand at this very spot to retrieve this magic coin. We hereby affix our signatures in blood."

Carrie also had with her a wooden pencil box that contained several kitchen matches and a darning needle wrapped in gauze. I lit one of the matches and tried to hold it steady as Carrie proceeded to sterilize the needle. On the first try the needle turned purple, then blue, then a brilliant yellow-red before she dropped it. The second time, she held it with the gauze. When I jabbed her finger, Carrie shut her eyes tightly and winced. She could not bring herself to prick my finger, and so, with great bravado, I did my own, although I too winced. When attempts to write our signatures in blood failed, we resigned ourselves to dabbing our fingers on the card and scrawling our names below the marks in pencil. We removed the loose stone from our secret place—the sixteenth stone from the west corner of the wall and the third one up—and carefully stashed the card behind it.

THE CHATTERING OF Nurse Bundy's stainless steel cart as it navigates the corridor with its cargo of meds jolts me back to Pineview. It's seven a.m., plenty of time to walk the two miles into town. Slipping out is really easy what with the turnover of personnel and all, each batch dumber than the last.

Used to be I could thumb it into Centerville, but now with traffic moving so fast, it's dangerous. So I hug the curbs and navigate entrances and exits as best I can, sucking in fumes and flipping birdies at irate drivers—something I never would have done when I was younger. I figure I have about half an hour before I'm missed and have to stick to the shadows.

As I cling to the shoulder, I spot a single yellow rose poking through asphalt. You'd never know there used to be a row of houses here behind a picket fence but for that pathetic flower gasping for survival, which tells me I'm on the very spot that was Miss March's garden. "March the Marm" we called her. All she ever loved was that garden and her students.

∽✑✑

IT WAS A FRIDAY, collection day, and I handed Miss March a clean *Centerville Courier*—one from the middle of my bag. "And this is for you, Geoffrey," she said, handing me a shiny new quarter. It was a weekly ritual, this exchange, and I knew that I was one of her few indulgences. As I turned to leave, I shifted the canvas strap, which had been digging into my shoulder, to the other side and adjusted the bag for balance.

∽✑✑

THE PICKET FENCE IS GONE, and I'm back on the shoulder staring at the rose. Its petals flutter in the wake of a passing truck and, too weak to hang on to its stem, they gust into the path of yet another vehicle and disappear beneath its wheels in an eddying swirl, a strange dance of death.

I fight my way across the street, a two-step process, to the concrete median where I hesitate as a driver looks at me as if to say "make my day." And I've half a mind to do just that...to sacrifice myself to call his bluff—perhaps as good a way to go as any.

When I reach the other side, I duck into Bass Brothers Hardware, which is still there, although it's now Ace.

∽✑✑

ED AND HENRY BASS were identical, both skinny and bald, but easy to tell apart because Ed talked too much and Henry not enough, as if he'd ceded his tongue to his twin. But what Ed didn't know, Henry did—it was just harder to get it from him, prying out monosyllables and all. One morning, I dealt with Ed, trying to get what I needed for my Soapbox Derby entry. All I wanted to know was how to get the wheels on right, but Ed was hell-bent on explaining the mechanics of ball bearings, friction, and such. When he was finally lectured out, he turned to an elderly lady who'd been tugging at his sleeve.

⁓◉〜

LIKE MISS MARCH'S GARDEN, the big brass cash register with its embossed pattern has disappeared—in its place is a computer, behind which sits a pimply-faced kid in a red vest with an Ace logo over the pocket. You can tell just by looking at him that he wouldn't know a gasket from a six-penny nail.

I step back into the street and continue my trek toward Locust, stopping beneath the awning of Flink's Pharmacy to peer through the window.

⁓◉〜

BEHIND THE SODA FOUNTAIN COUNTER, I filled the reservoir with Coca-Cola syrup. Kay Star's voice blared from the jukebox: "Oh, we ain't got a barrel of money..." The place was abuzz with kids just out of school. A couple at the end of the counter shared a banana split, both giggling as they use the same spoon: a vicarious adolescent soul kiss. "Maybe we're ragged and funny..." Morton Flink stayed in the back room, annoyed by the daily hormone-driven turmoil of teens and their crazy music. "But we're traveling along, singing a song..." Yet he was all too aware that without the nickels pumped into the ghastly machine with its bubbling colored lights and rotating platters, without the gallons of cherry cokes and milkshakes, business would not be the same.

"Side by side."

⁓◉〜

THE VISION makes me thirsty. I fumble in my pockets for the dollar bill I've been hiding from the Pineview staff. I rub my eyes. The jukebox is gone, the kids are gone, even the fountain is gone, and in its place stretch endless racks of DVDs and CDs.

I continue down Main to the corner of Locust where there's a traffic light; one of four where there used to be only stop signs. I turn west on Locust, heading smack-dab into the blinding late-afternoon sun. The rows of trees that lined both sides of the street have been removed and replaced with parking meters. The old slate sidewalks have been skinnied down to narrow ribbons of concrete, and I wonder why, if they've gone that far, they just don't take it all and be done with it. I'm suddenly shaken by an ear-piercing din, and as I round the curve, I encounter its source—a jagged-toothed yellow Caterpillar backhoe perched above the steps.

Both houses are gone. My father's and the Spangler's. Only the retaining wall remains with its majestic granite steps which look ridiculous leading up to nothing...nothing but rubble and a myriad of twisted memories.

I follow the length of the wall, my hand tingling as it moves along the top. I don't have to count the stones; I could do this blindfolded. I reach the loose stone and caress it with trembling fingertips. It is not yet time. I must wait for sunset...and for Carrie.

I work my way back to the base of the steps and notice that the numbers 327, once so faded you could hardly see them, have been repainted, and the 7, which always leaned a little to the left, has been straightened and moved closer to the 2.

The sun slips lower now, and the lengthening shadows, unlike the ones I remember so vividly, sweep aimlessly across a mass of debris. The noise has stopped, replaced by voices of men in hardhats laughing and rattling their empty lunch buckets.

I'm hungry and tired, so I sit leaning against the granite column. I hunker in the shadows, heart pounding, cheek nuzzled against the steps.

~◎~

CARRIE is counting...

"Ollie, Ollie infantry, here I come, ready or not!"

~◎~

I PRESS MY LIPS against the warm stone and close my eyes to make myself invisible, the penny slipping from my hand. ◆

143

TOMATOES

My mother raised her children
the same way she raised her prize-winning tomatoes.
Digging a hole,
she planted them deep in the ground,
nearby she placed a bucket half full of bullshit.
If they seemed to wane,
she scooped rainwater off of the manure
and poured it around them,
in a wide circle to protect their tender roots.
As they grew, she visited them daily,
watching their growth,
checking their leaves for diseases or parasites.
Using soft linen rags, ripped by her long thin fingers,
she tied their branches to a frame,
to help support the weight on their young limbs
and train them to stand tall.
When her fruit fell from the vine green,
she scooped them off the ground,
dusted them off,
and placed them in a sunny kitchen window.
There, under her watchful eye,
they ripened slowly,
till their skin was thick but tender,
and inside they were just the right mixture
of sweet and tart.
Then, with a small smile,
she served them up to the world.

MY ALBERTA

You are the only one left.

Struggling to stay green,
surrounded by wilting geraniums,
scrawny Bradford pears,
omens of unfulfilled prophecies,
never to bow with abundance.

According to shopping serendipity,
you are meant to go home with me, but first
I must carry you to a shopping cart,
maneuver up and down grocery aisles,
blind spots blocked by green branches,
a future filled with birds and growth.

You look better already, towering over
green olives, ripe tomatoes, wheat bread and honey,
foreshadowing sustenance, like the woman who comments
how lovely you will look come Christmas,
our eyes glistening like jelly jars, bright with possibility.
At the checkout, when the cashier asks: *Is that a tree?*
I want to say, "No, this is my grandmother,
Alberta Maybelle Porter," but maybe
he has not read Faulkner, is a stranger to the logic of grief,
games it plays with love and longing.
On the back floorboard you ride comfortably,
while I practice a lifetime of conversation, small talk

grown large with the significance of never having been spoken:
Do you like this song?
Are you hungry?
Mmm, you smell so good.
Hey! Look! There's Linda and Danny!
When they pull up hollering out rolled down windows
I want to ease up a little further, point proudly and ask:
See my Alberta?

They would smile knowing and not knowing.
Here in this almost intersection convergence
of three poets and a stalled train, anything is possible.
This is my grandmother.
We are heading home.

SAVAGE GULF
by Matt Forsythe

Stacy Jones

Sears Wish Book:
A Staple of
Rural Southern Childhood

Sometime in August of each year, the delivery of the mail brought a mainstay of rural childhood, a most valuable book, a provision of hours of delight, an object that spurred pure desire, sheer lust. The thing came wrapped discreetly in brown paper, but we children knew what it was when our mailboxes bulged with its weight.

The arrival of the Sears Wish Book in August gave us roughly four months to pour over its slick pages hour upon hour, leafing through the plethora of toys, folding down corners, and carefully noting with magic marker the selections we hoped to discover under our Christmas trees that fabled, long-awaited morning.

The images on the cover were comforting, typifying a traditional middle class suburban holiday. The cover presented a myriad of nostalgia-laden imagery, involving some combination of a Christmas tree, a fireplace, Santa Claus, and children, usually pajama-clad and filled with wonder over both the presents left under the tree and the snow falling gently outside the window.

Although my literal experience of Christmas was a bit different from the imagery depicted on the cover, I still related to it somehow. Of course, I had no fireplace in my house—a fact that posed a slight problem when I was younger, as I'm sure it does with many a child, when the question arose as to how exactly Santa gained entry to the living room. Snow rarely fell in southwest Tennessee, and when it did, it was usually in January or February, long after the last shred of holiday tinsel was to be found. We also didn't have a tree that looked as though it had been professionally decorated; a simple cedar plucked from the woods behind our house and decorated by my brother and me sufficed. Furthermore, as for pajamas, I didn't usually wear anything akin to the cozy, one-piece red or green outfits that adorned the children who posed as models on the cover.

I suppose I was caught up, as most children are, in the romanticism of Christmas. Even if my life wasn't exactly like that of those children on the front cover, it was still an idyllic existence to be able to spend time dreaming about the possibilities. And looking back, I think the dreaming may have been as much fun—perhaps even more sometimes—than the getting.

In my reverie, I was fascinated by almost all of the toys in the book, from Barbie dolls to Hot Wheels, from Cabbage Patch Kids to chemistry sets. Fortunately, my parents never refused to let me play with certain toys, or encouraged me to play with other ones, simply because I was a girl. And so I didn't feel limited by my choices, as long as the cost wasn't too extravagant.

Every year around the middle of December, I reverently made my pilgrimage to our local Sears catalog store to visit with Santa and submitted my long-considered request. Because of these obvious connections between Sears and the holiday, at a young age I may well have thought that Sears & Roebuck invented Christmas. One particular year, though, I made the definite transition from innocence to experience when our preacher posed as Santa for the store, confirming my growing suspicions that the jolly old fellow might not be real, as least not in the way I had always been told or imagined. At any rate, Christmas without Sears would have been a very different one indeed, and the two will probably always be indelibly connected in my memory.

Of course, Sears discontinued its catalog business in 1992, the same year I suffered the death of my father, and I connect both events with the beginnings of my adulthood. And, despite my realization that I was part of a generation most assuredly marked by consumerism, I still feel a twinge for those who will never know the joys of long hours spent with the Sears Wish Book, dreaming, imagining, even in the absence of such, a crackling fire and snow falling on long winter afternoons. ◆

Stephen Roger Powers

ONLY $2 TO SEE THE WORLD'S LARGEST MODEL RAILROAD DISPLAY!

Chattanooga, Tennessee

Go there. You'll see
little houses, little hills,
little cars, little redbud trees,
little bears, little wash
lines. The little plastic
people look like they'll burst
alive in Halloos and Howdys
and Nice-to-See-Yas
and clog dancing.
If you peek really close, down
in the corner, near the end
of the World's Largest Model
Railroad Display, you'll even see a little
person (maybe she's a little
girl and her name is Wanda
Parlapiano) diving into a little
swimming pool, little legs sticking out
of the little glassy fake water
like the ends of broken hairpins.
There I decided on my new
hobby—model Dollywooding.
I will build the World's
Largest Model Dollywood

Only $2 to See the World's Largest Model Railroad Display!

Display, complete with working
steam train, parking lot,
trash collection service,
bluegrass theater, backporch
ham & beans restaurant with
pie tins, fruit jars, and picnic tables,
lye soap stand, kiddie tree house,
homemade candle store, sausages
frying, little ducks quacking
in spring rain puddles, season
pass photo booth, and maybe
even a tiny little miniature Dolly
Parton on a buggy that putts
through the miniature park
as she waves to all the little fans
that are too small to paint faces on.

Kay Newton

FOLLY ISLAND, AUGUST

My name is April, but I call myself Augusta,
for my favorite month, when Daddy brings me here
to the beach. It's lucky I'm home-schooled; my mom
thinks school should never start before September.
I love it here, I love this time of year,
and this year, next year, and forever after,
I'll love Charles, my very distant cousin,
who's staying in the cottage next to ours.
His mom and dad, like mine, are from Valdosta,
but they've lived in Paris, France, for years,
and that's where Charles was born. I know he's fourteen
and too old for me—I'm almost twelve—
and, *c'est dommage,* he's wild about Maureen,
my dad's new wife, who's come with us this year
for her first time. I hate her. So does Winona,
our Welsh corgi, who is smart. Last year,
I didn't love Charles—I was still in love
with Mike, back home, who moved to Arizona
for his asthma. He was my age. If he
loved me back, he never let me know.
He left; I came here to the beach heartbroken.
Quelle surprise! Charles, my short fat cousin,
has improved in just a year! Presto!
He's six feet tall, at least, and so good-looking—
he has curly hair all over, and it gleams
like copper wire against his tan. His teeth
could be a toothpaste ad, and when he talks,

he doesn't make those high-pitched squeaks
at unexpected moments. He's not perfect—
no help at all at hunting hermit crabs
and wouldn't touch the blue-tailed skink I caught.
But he no longer hits and teases me
and hasn't pulled my ponytail one time,
and when I swallowed too much ocean once,
he put his arm around me while I coughed;
and when my chest, so tender since my "rosebuds
started blooming" (as Mom puts it), brushed
against his arm as we picked muscadines,
it didn't hurt, but made me feel all flushed
and funny. Don't tell, but yesterday I found him
sleeping in the hammock on the porch—
the grown-ups had gone fishing, left him here
to baby-sit—and I snuck up and kissed him
right on the lips as he was lying there.
His eyes, green as the sea, went wide, surprised,
but he smiled sleepily and mussed my hair.
"Hey, kid, what's up?' he said. "Don't call me kid!"
"Okay, kid"—but he pulled me down beside him.
We swung together till we got all sweaty,
then raced down to the water to cool off.
By Monday he'll be back in France already,
and I'll go back to Mama's in Valdosta.
I don't care. I'll love him all year long,
count down the days, and call myself Augusta.

THE GIFT

Empty packs of Tareytons carpeted
the rusted floor-boards of my sister's car,
"White Trash." Cigarette butts, gum wrappers,

and wadded up pop quizzes tossed about
the 1957 Olds like balls in a bingo machine.
Out of the air you might pluck a translation

from *The Iliad*, Hector dragging Achilles
by the heel around the fields of Troy or
Cassandra's unheeded warning to beware

of Greeks bearing gifts. A not-quite-empty can
of Schlitz and a leaky bottle of Neatsfoot oil
gurgled over a mud-caked horse blanket, the heap

smoldering on the backseat like the remains of Troy
as the Greeks sailed quickly away. When she graduated
from high school, my sister handed me the keys

to White Trash, an archeological dig in motion,
honking at every right turn, lurching past revved-up
Chevys with a mere nudge to the accelerator.
It was a bequest I both loved and feared,
as I did my sister, soon to be a 'white' Black Panther
wanting to kill all the capitalists, including our father,

a Knoxville merchant. She could spot someone's
fatal flaw (not whispered in her ear by some
jealous god) instantly, especially the eagerness

of a sister holding out both hands for a gift,
now a trusted knight with keys to her salvation.

justin.barrett

i was a third grade genius

in third grade
we were forced
to take IQ tests
to be certain
that none of us were
too far off the
scale,
one way or the
the other.

it just so happened that
i tested in
the genius range.

i was bumped up to
advanced classes
and made to read all
manner of
difficult books
full of symbolism
and foreshadowing.

i was coddled and
fawned over
by my teachers and
parents as they
tried to protect and nurture

the delicate genius
that lay inside me,
but
things didn't work
out as everyone
had hoped.

today, i am a
struggling poet and
a struggling
factory worker who
is no longer coddled
or nurtured,

who still
looks upon the world
through the eyes
of a third grade
genius.

5TH AVENUE: MOVE OUT DAY
by Catie Tappan

Rebecca K. Brooks

A Hot, Gray Day

*I*t's hot, and I'm driving to the funeral of Norma's father. The piece of paper with the directions slides onto the floor as I swerve on a curve on US Route 316. *Heck.* I pull on the collar of my white blouse under my black funeral suit as I look for a place to pull over. There's a long hill ahead, and the four cylinders in my trusty white Volvo feel the tug. Over the hill, I see a wide spot in the road before the next curve. I seek out a new radio station—the easy listening station disappeared in the last valley. *Nothing but country preaching.* I rummage around in my purse for the pill bottle, steering with one hand. At the wide spot, I retrieve the directions and pour out a handful of pills. *Blue or green? I think I took green this morning—I should take blue now.* I feel better immediately as I gulp the blues down with a bottle of Coke.

Ahead, the road straightens in a deep gorge and I see another long pull ahead. *Jeeeez. I should have brought the Mercedes. Then I would at least have fun on this road. Norma was right when she said it was in the mountains.* The directions say New Holiness Vision Church is about one mile on the left past Homer's Grocery. The store should be coming up soon. I see it on the right, just a wide place with an old building perched on the side of the hill. On impulse, I pull into the parking lot—my Coke is getting hot. There's a scruffy old hound dog lying square in front of the door.

"Hello doggy," I say, not taking my eyes off of the dog. "Move, doggy." The dog doesn't move. "Hello. Anybody there?"

Someone starts to open the door from the inside, and the dog jumps up and runs across the road to the porch of an old trailer. A man in a

159

baseball hat with greasy hair hanging out the sides says, "Howdy, ma'am."

My eyes are focused on his shirt—a red flannel with the sleeves cut out, unbuttoned to his bulging belly. He sees me looking, and I think that he thinks I am looking at him with lust. *Just go to the bathroom and get my Coke and get out of here fast*, I tell myself.

"What 'cha doin' in these parts?" he asks politely. It's then I notice he has about five teeth.

"Excuse me," I say and hurry into the store.

Inside, a fat lady sits behind the counter in a blue house-dress with her hair rolled up in pink sponge rollers. A 1962 calendar depicting a little girl praying hangs beside a 1999 calendar advertising Smith Funeral Home. What did these people do between those years? Two other men are leaning on the counter, watching me step carefully around a second dog in front of the counter.

"Do you have a restroom?" I ask.

"We have a commode," she says, "back there through that door."

I go through a door with a hand-lettered sign: *Private. Do not Enter.* A low watt bulb dimly lights the restroom. The small room, once pink, has now taken on the hue of faintly pink dirt. I carefully try to not touch anything. I look around for tissue but find none. A once-pink cloth towel hangs on the towel bar, and the sign above the bar reads: *We will close this bathroom if you don't keep it clean.* I rummage through my purse for tissue. There's no water from the sink faucets. *Haven't these people heard of toilet paper and paper towels.* I'm glad that I live far away.

Back in the store, I look around for the coolers with Coke. Seeing none, I finally ask.

"They're in the 'frige."

I get my canned Coke, checking it for an expiration date.

"You from 'round here?" the lady asks.

"No."

"Where you from?" she says.

"Knoxville. I'm here for a funeral," I say, wondering why I allowed myself to disclose such information.

"You family?"

I just answer her no and then quickly go out the door. The two men follow me to the door and watch me get in the car.

Back on the road, I think about my unlikely friendship with Norma. She's unpretentious, something I never learned to be. She's not my mother, but she is a mother type. I can't imagine Norma telling me at dinner every other night that I must never cry when I am sad. "It breeds weakness," Mother would say. Norma quietly induced me to cry on her shoulder one day when I ran into her in a department store. My boyfriend had just broken up with me by cell phone. I was flitting from cosmetic counter to perfume counter when she spotted me. She was so glad to see me. Tissue magically appeared, and she hugged me and told me to let it all come out. It was comforting.

Some evenings with Mother, it was difficult just to get through dinner: "Margaret, do not use your salad fork for your vegetables." I hated the way Margaret sounded—everyone else, including Daddy, called me Maggie.

❦

I MET NORMA when I was a struggling second-year attorney, working for an even more-struggling law firm. They gave me the cases no one else wanted. Norma walked in and declared to the receptionist: "I need a lawyer," and according to previous instruction, the receptionist sent her to me. I half-heartedly took down the facts of her case, that her mother died two months ago, her father was in a nursing home, and her four brothers were selling "hairlooms" out of the family home. "Could you please stop them?" she asked, and I said I would review the case and call her. I took three months to call and tell her we had a court date, and I showed up thirty minutes late after a long night of watching black and white movies on TV. I held my breath for at least fifteen minutes until I learned the case hadn't been called yet. My black suit soaked up gallons of sweat while I sat there hoping my ten 'til midnight discovery of the obscure *Pickett v. Pickett* in 1993 was the correct precedent. I couldn't believe my luck when the judge ruled for Norma; unbeknownst to me, the judge was the one who argued *Pickett* before the Tennessee Supreme Court, and of course, he very much agreed with me. Norma's brothers stood like trees beside the opposing attorney, and we left the courthouse under four pairs of eyes that reminded me of the mafia, a subject I only knew about from late-night TV. They lined up in ascending order of body weight from left to right, all of them dressed in black suits and red ties, all of them glaring at me as Norma hugged me, saying she would never forget me. I stifled a small guilt for the fee, knowing I had spent all of fifteen minutes preparing the case. After that, Norma called me regularly and asked me to lunch.

She worked at a little florist's in Oak Ridge. One warm day on a whim, I took my 1988 red 560 Mercedes with its meager five thousand miles, which Daddy had given me when I passed the bar, and picked her up. We drove around for two hours with the top down, past two of her brothers' houses, past the house of the niece who had been calling her on the phone and leaving dirty messages and finally to the garage where her husband worked. He walked around the car with his face beaming as he studied its shape.

"Ain't it pretty?" Norma said.

"It sure is. What year is it?" he asked.

I told him all I knew about the car and asked if he wanted to drive it. He declined but Norma and I rode around for a while longer before I left her at the florist's, smiling.

〜❧〜

I WONDER HOW FAR I AM from Pulpton and the New Holiness Vision Church when an old pickup truck that looks like it's been dying for ten years pulls out in front of me going thirty-five miles an hour while I impatiently tap my foot on the gas pedal, hoping to floor it on a straightaway. There is none, but soon the truck turns left without a signal onto a side road, and I once again push the cylinders in my Volvo to their limit. Finally, at the top of the hill, I see a red brick church. The sign outside confirms that I'm in the right place, and I pull into a parking spot. I take a minute to fix my lipstick, my hair and brush the lint off my suit. I go up the steps, hoping the church has air-conditioning as the heat creeps quickly through my suit. Both front doors are open, and I immediately see several ladies fanning away the offensive July heat.

Norma stands at the right of the coffin, and the four brothers are stationed with their wives on the left. There's a line of about twelve people waiting to speak to the family, and I get in the back. *I must be early*, I think, checking my watch. *One-fifteen. Heck. I've got forty-five minutes to wait.* Norma sees me, leaves her obligatory spot and rushes over to hug me.

"You've got to stand up here with me," she says, taking my hand and leading me over to her space.

In a small moment, I find myself receiving friends of the deceased, none of whom I know. People are shaking my hand, saying they are sorry for my loss, and I wonder how I got into this situation. What in my life brought me to this place at this particular time? After four or five people, I fall right into the part, saying "thank you" and "I'm so glad you could come" and "he thought a lot of you, too" and other phrases that I had never used because I had never stood in a funeral line. Between the mourners, I look out into the audience, expecting to see Rod Serling in gray tones sitting somewhere near the back of the church with his head leaning slightly to the right. Instead, I see the fat lady from the store, only her rollers are gone and tight curls cover her head, and she has changed her blue house-dress for a black caftan. My hand is being squeezed over and over, I am hugging old women who smell of warm lavender powder and I am trying not to notice the four brothers who each have looked at me twice with steel eyes floating in moisture.

At five minutes to two, as if staged perfectly, the mourners all sit down suddenly, the choir comes in, the mafia-looking funeral directors quietly but firmly lead the family to their seats and I whisper to Norma that I will sit in the back. She hooks her arm in mine and says, "No, you sit with me," and I am led to the front row where I sit on one side, her husband on the other.

Behind us sit the four brothers, two of them weeping because the coffin has been closed, and just before the choir begins singing "Blessed Assurance" in a timid off-key, I hear the next-to-biggest brother sniffle to his wife, "Family's supposed to sit here." I sink in my seat and venture a side glance at Norma. She is dry-eyed and glowing proudly like a recital mom rather than a grieving daughter.

The choir sits down and one of the ministers comes to the pulpit and gives the eulogy. *I hope this is going to be short.* He leads a long prayer, praying for every citizen in Pulpton by name. He sits down, and from the back of the choir loft, a man in a tight, white shirt and dark tie with his hair still damp from being recently slicked down comes to the pulpit. He sings a haunting song, a cappella, with a voice that is country and good and genuine. His face is familiar, and I catch my breath a little when I realize he's the man from the store with the five teeth.

"He's my cousin Jimmy," Norma whispers.

Another minister gets up and begins telling how well he knew the deceased and how much a witness his life had been. *OK, this is going pretty fast.* I sit up a little in my seat to look around a bit, checking my watch, thinking I could be back in Knoxville by four. I am enjoying the flowers, at least, breathing in their subtle scent, when suddenly my head jerks up as if one of the brothers had me on a puppet string. My eyes are mesmerized by the minister's beet-red face, sweat dripping from his cheeks; he catches the sweat every fifteen seconds or so with a huge white handkerchief. His eyes bulge like the Taco Bell dog, his Bible dangles in his left hand and his right hand pounds the pulpit with his left hand on the up-swing, making him look like a soldier hoping to surrender. My mouth opens, and it is not until five minutes later that I remember to shut it.

The minister has begun a blazing missive in a voice that I am sure will cause Norma's father to sit up in the coffin and any babies asleep in a two-mile radius to suddenly awaken from their naps.

"And I tell you brothers-uh, and sisters-uh, that if you don't depart-uh, from your evil ways-uh, that you are-uh, all doomed for hell-uh. Hell that is hot-uh, hotter than that sun out there today-uh, hotter than your cookstove was this morning-uh, hotter than anything-uh you can imagine-uh. And you'll be down there-uh, begging for some water-uh, and this man here-uh, he'll be in heaven-uh, and he won't be able to give you water-uh, and you'll burn in hell forever-uh."

With each little "uh," his voice goes up several pitches, and I realize after a minute or so that the "uh" is his breath. This goes on for twenty more minutes, and I turn around a little, avoiding the brothers' eyes, looking in the back for *something*—something I don't know except maybe from my other life. By three-fifteen, I have transported myself into semi-sleep, and suddenly Norma is nudging me to stand, the choir is singing a final lament, and we walk out as a family, me carefully avoiding the sorrowful eyes of neighbors and friends, looking forward to the refuge of my Volvo.

Outside, Norma says, "You're staying for the burial, aren't you?"

I fumble for the words. "Uh, I need to get back. I don't think I can."

She says, "We're all going down the mountain to my house afterwards. There's lots of food. Can't you stay?"

I look at the Volvo. A distant city calls to me. "No, I have to get back. I have an appointment." *That always works*, I think, *appointments are important*. She hugs me anyway, and I get into the car, turning the air on high, not bothering to open the windows to let out some of the heat. As I back out, I see next-to-smallest brother scowling at me from the church steps.

On the road I let down the windows, loving the air that blows my hair into tangles. The words from Jimmy's song reverberate in my head:

With friends on earth we meet in gladness
While swift the moments fly
Yet ever comes the tho't of sadness
That we must say 'goodbye'
We'll never say goodbye in heaven
For in that land of joy and song
We'll never say goodbye.

I'm five miles from the Twilight Zone by now, and up ahead, there's a wide edge on the road, enough to turn around. I dig through my purse for the paper, looking for directions to the cemetery. Then I remember that the cemetery was behind the church with a pretty picket fence around it. I had seen a gray funeral tent freshly erected on the left side of the cemetery.

The wide shoulder is a pull-off for motorists to look at the view, and for the first time, I look at the scenery. I am high enough that in the distance I recognize the gray haze of the Smoky Mountains. There is a river snaking through a gorge to the left, and houses dot the landscape, looking as if a small boy had flung them down carelessly in his play. ◆

Teresa Joy Kramer

GREENS AND BROWNS

The greens and browns of this
pre-teen's flip-flops are lighter
than the tones of earth in wet spring.
She angles her rubber sandals
to tamp down the seeds.
Her toes slide as she works—
the little one slips entirely
off the edge, into wet dirt;
the next one hugs her sandal's
half-inch rubber.

She straightens, taps the hoe
against her palm, and says:
We're going to have lots of surprises
this summer.

Mud is creeping up over *The Gap*
and between all of her toes—longer
this year, almost adult-size.
By mid-morning, the caked brown
is half-dried and half-dark.

Don Williams

HER VAGABOND NEON-HEART

Loretta Garner drew a scarlet scarf over scarlet lips and lightly freckled nose, then gazed at me with emerald eyes and became someone new. Familiar with her penchant for drama, I never paid the performance due attention, as she affected a nasal, French accent and warned me, "I could be anyone, *monsieur*. From now on...*a partir d'aujourd d'hui...appelez-moi...um, Loretta Dupree.*"

I laughed at her faltering French, swirled the amber and ice in my tumbler and said, "Only if you call me Napoleon Bonaparte."

She dropped her veil, pulled a barrette from her auburn hair and shook it out, and when she spoke, she did so in the hillbilly voice that always returned after two fingers of sherry.

"Napoleon Bonaparte. Hah. You don't have the imagination for it, Counselor."

That's what she called me when I disappointed her, which I did ever more frequently.

"On the other hand...*regardez-moi!* I have the ability to alter my whole identity, my whole life."

"Sure you do," I said, "Marry me."

She sat back and gazed at me, assessing intentions, possibilities. "That'll be the day," she muttered at last, then drained her glass. But I see now, as I watch the planes taxiing onto the runway, that she was torn. I all but had her before the justice of the peace, or before the stained glass of St. John's Cathedral, dear God, had I pressed for a verdict, but I never did and, for her part, she never said yes.

Still, there were signs of hope. The pauses before no had lately grown longer. I wasn't fool enough to think it was because she loved me. I knew even then she mostly loved herself, just as I knew that if she married me, it would be because there were only two games in town for Loretta Garner. One of them was *The News-Pulse*, where she wrote edgy features about the city's rich and powerful. The other game was me, and I was confident enough to believe I could always hold her, not only because our love-making was frequent and good, but because I knew how she loved all the props and sets, the sounds and costumes of affluence and power against which the our romance played itself out. She loved the smell of calfskin leather upholstery in my office, the feel of silk and woolen suits, the warm blush of imported sherry. She loved to ratchet up Mendelssohn or Merle Haggard on my high-tech stereo as she admired my Chippendale desk, the decorative writing plumes in porcelain inkwells, the ancient volumes in my library.

As I said, Loretta also loved drama, and as a trial lawyer, I knew how to provide it. She thrilled to the adrenaline surge in the courtroom when an unfriendly witness would answer a question just a heartbeat before realizing I'd used his own words to expose a flaw at the heart of the prosecutor's case. She kept a change of clothes in my office, so we could shower and go to dinner and the movies afterwards. Back at my apartment, we would make love if the film had put her in a good mood. An ancient, sentimental gem like *Casablanca* or *It Happened One Night* would do nicely.

Our affair was going, if not well, at least predictably—in an ordered ebb and flow that appealed to my temperament. I appreciated order, decorum, in those days. It's why I'd signed on with Wilson, Remington and Bryant. The moment I walked between the twin columns at the doorstep and into their symmetrical spaces, the world made sense. Despite the messiness of my clients' lives, my life became a continuous cycle of procedure and drama. Loretta blended nicely with that routine.

It never occurred to me she might want out, even though she was frustrated with our town. I assumed her dissatisfaction was rooted in her job. She was a secret critic of print journalism, a profession run by an unholy alliance of young marketing execs and newspaper editors who tended to cut her prose like a rope when space was tight. I thought, mistakenly, I see now, that her dissatisfaction would draw her closer to me, and so

I secretly savored those complaints about her job, even when pretending not to.

"They try and make me write my stories upside down and backwards," she said as we sat in Club Manhattan, "Hit the reader with a two-by-four in the first sentence, then let it peter off to nothing." Again, it was the mountain girl speaking. She gulped her sherry. "I have too many bosses, dammit, and all they want to do is become *USA Today* and turn anybody who can write into a keypunch operator. Well, not Loretta Garner. I'm leaving."

"Where will you go?" We both knew the town's afternoon paper had closed two years before.

"I don't know—somewhere. Maybe I'll get out of newspapers for good. Start over." That's when she pulled her red scarf over her face and changed her voice. I often think of that moment.

∽◎◦

IN OUR SECOND SPRING TOGETHER she won the University of Michigan Journalism Fellowship, one of those programs that every bored or rebellious journalist who makes a big enough mark applies for sooner or later. She brought her letter of acceptance by in late afternoon. I had a client in the office, one Jefferson Wu. Along with sixteen other mostly-ethnics whose houses were being condemned for a flood control project, Wu had defied the order to move. It was a high-profile case, and I made Loretta wait her turn. If there was one principle to which I adhered in this business, it was that the client always comes first. That was the difference between Wilson, Remington and Bryant and the pretenders in this town. Besides, I couldn't have Jefferson knowing a reporter was horning in on our appointment.

After seeing Mr. Wu out, I poured myself a Scotch, a fine, single-malt Scotch, and sat alone for two minutes considering what tack to take with Loretta. I felt my detachment soften as the whiskey warmed my belly, and I found myself wondering whether a dramatic proposal of marriage might stop her from leaving. Still irresolute, I summoned her. She wore a silken white blouse and green hound's tooth skirt over nylons that glistened. Her hair was incandescent under office lights and her skin alabaster white. I saw anew that she was gorgeous.

She waved the document before my eyes and adopted a Deep South accent to mask her nervous hillbilly soul. "If you would be so kind, *suh,*" she said. She sat down and watched me pour amber sherry into crystal and pass it to her. She nodded her thanks and muttered the Vivien Leigh line from *Streetcar,* "I have always depended on the kindness of *strangers.*"

I let the reproach pass and read the document aloud, starting with the part that thanked her for her interest in the mid-career program, and she snatched the sheet from me.

"What do they mean mid-career? I'm twenty-seven."

"Almost twenty-eight," I said, laughing at her vanity. Then I explained the fine print. How Michigan U would provide a substantial stipend so that for nine months she could study anything she wanted. Three obligations were at the heart of the document. She must write nothing for publication during her fellowship. She must attend twice-weekly seminars featuring such notables as Mike Wallace and Ben Bradlee, and she must sign a pledge to return to her job after the fellowship year.

"Why is that last part in there?" she asked in a voice straight out of the Kentucky hills, so I knew she meant business. I made a fatal error, I see now, by answering honestly.

"That clause is strictly non-binding. Ignore it." I tossed the letter into her lap, then knelt on one knee and put my hands on her trim waist. Her mingled fragrances made me feverish with longing, and my right hand slid to the mother-of-pearl buttons on her blouse. She didn't stop me exactly. She merely picked up the letter even as I leaned over and nuzzled her neck.

"How d'ya figure?" she asked, tilting the crown of her head toward mine to protect the pale flesh of her neck from my lips. I lifted my face from the wildwood fragrance of her hair. "How can it be *non-binding?* I have to promise I'll come back."

"The reason it's ... non-binding," I said, as I pulled the blouse from her skirt, "is because what we have here is a third-party agreement. You have a pact with the university that you'll return, and the paper has a pact with them that it will take you back. All of which puts you in the catbird's seat."

I unfastened her bra, cupped a white breast in my warm right hand, but she stood abruptly.

"How does that put me in the catbird's seat?"

"Simple." I stood as quickly as I could do so with dignity. "The paper would never break its agreement with Michigan to take you back because it would appear foolish and dishonest," I said, exasperated. "But if *you* break your agreement to come back to the paper, Michigan won't bother to go to the expense of enforcing it. Even if they did, I would handle your case pro bono."

She pegged across the room, still in her heels, her lovely pale breasts framed by the twin curtains of her opened blouse. She tossed back her sherry, then sat down in my Queen Anne chair and looked out at the city. "You could change your whole life," she said, with awe at the sudden revelation.

"Sure you could. Come here."

She came to me then and we made love, a triumphant, dramatic act starring Loretta Dupree.

⌘

WHEN LORETTA LEFT for Ann Arbor that September, her car held a sleeping bag, an end table she had stolen from the first apartment she ever rented, a box of old movies I had recorded for her, assorted music, and clothes, makeup and accoutrements. She left in the evening to keep from disrupting my workday, she said. She gave me a kiss that lingered, and then she was gone, into the purple dusk.

I was alone to establish new routines. In the evenings I would retire to Club Manhattan for cocktails and shoptalk. I tried going to the movies, but without the touch of nylon and lace beneath my hand, it wasn't the same. I began to look forward to her calls and other communiqués with a child-like anticipation that surprised me. Her first email set the tone.

⌘

Dearest Dewey,

It's like I've stepped through the Looking Glass here. Everyone's engaged in amazing things. Yesterday I met a carillonneur who goes hopscotching from town to town around the globe playing cathedral bells. Her bells ring across campus from a tall tower every hour. Young graduate students–writers and actors and artists and philosophers– are everywhere. There's a great little club on State Street that features jazz in the afternoon. Some of us Journalism Fellows (impressive, no?) had dinner with Mike Wallace last evening. He is quite the bon vivant in person, and he makes TV sound attractive. He says that with my voice and looks, and my "flair for the dramatic" (his words) I could have a future in broadcasting if I wanted it. But I don't know. I'm relieved not to be writing all those articles.

Just for fun, I'm taking this wonderful survey course on American film. I get to watch great movies like "Dr. Zhivago" and "Citizen Kane," on a big screen. Did you know that Rosebud was the pet name William Randolph Hearst gave to his mistress's pussy? At least that's what our professor said. It's one of the reasons Hearst wanted to shut the movie down.

Oh I miss you baby. I had forgotten how good we had it. When I got here I had no power, which meant no lights. I thought of splurging for new furniture, but I'll put that off and live like a vagabond student for a while. I bought a second-hand desk. The place had a dresser, a table and three chairs. The bed was rickety, so I had the landlady haul it off. I'm sleeping on a mattress on the floor, which wouldn't bother me if only you were here.

Love you Honeybee.

Yours, Loretta

P.S. How come you never give names to my privates? Tsk. Tsk. No imagination.

⤳⊙↶

I FILED THE MESSAGE AWAY and waited for the next.

It was a several weeks before the pattern of her studies emerged. Later emails mentioned Voice, Readings in Drama, Acting 101. I was amused to watch her facade of journalistic seriousness break down in Wonderland. God only knew what she would tell her editors when they asked how she was spending her time. For now it didn't matter. She was enjoying life. When she called to tell me she'd landed a bit part in a student production of *Twelfth Night*, I went into the Old Town, where gentrification was bringing new life, and purchased a diamond ring—two carats, one for each year we'd been together—and surprised her by flying up for her final performance.

I carried the ring in my breast pocket on the plane to Detroit and the taxi ride to Ann Arbor. I left the taxi at a red-light three blocks from the theater and walked through random snowflakes among students half my age, past galleries and coffee shops and columns of Greco-Roman architecture on campus buildings.

The theater was outstanding, with acoustics that wafted the sound whole to my balcony seat. I almost missed her first stage appearance, distracting myself by reaching into my pocket to touch the cold facets of her ring, so that when she spoke her first line, I wasn't certain it was she.

After the play I met her backstage. She kissed me, smearing my face with makeup. I mentally peeled away the face paint and layers of her elaborate costume, a twentieth century interpretation of a sixteenth century Englishman's version of ancient Italian finery. Loretta was in there somewhere.

"Oh, come with me to the cast party," she said.

I searched her eyes. "Can't we be alone? I have to go home tomorrow."

"But you just got here."

"Darling, I have seventeen families counting on me to be in court Tuesday morning; we have only one night."

"Oh." She bit her lower lip, tore herself from my arms and passed herself around the room. The kisses from Antonio and Sebastian lasted longer than necessary, but I didn't say anything. They were mere boys, probably gay. She changed into jeans and a sweatshirt and we left arm in arm.

She was silent as we walked among haloed street lamps and confetti snow. On a dark side street, as snow whispered around us, we entered a two-story wood frame house. She led me up dusky twisting stairs to a door with chipped brown paint and into her apartment.

We made love with the strained urgency of strangers, and afterwards I held her in my arms and closed my eyes and tried to remember how it used to be. Later, we sat on her mattress beneath Japanese lanterns and ate Chinese food from little cartons. I talked and Loretta was quiet, her silence, I hoped, a sign of fascination at my accounts of cases on which I had been working, but when I stopped talking, silence yawned between us.

"Honey," she said at last. "How *was* I?"

"You know you're the best I ever had–"

"Not that, silly. I mean *on-stage.*"

"Oh...wonderful."

"Tell the truth."

"Terrific. Both lines...."

"Three. Four if you count the one delivered stage-right. I'll bet you don't remember any of my lines, do you, Counselor?"

I should have. I could recite half the script of *Casablanca*. Besides, close attention to fictitious performances was my stock in trade. I could see that a dramatic gesture was called for. "Let me consult my notes." I reached toward my jacket, which I'd placed across the back of a chair while undressing. My fingers dipped into my breast pocket and brought out the box containing the ring.

She stared at the little silvery case as she sat there in her robe among half-empty cartons of food. Then she reached one hand tentatively and took the box from me. She opened it. In the glow from paper lanterns her eyes moistened, but I couldn't read those tears.

~◈~

CHRISTMAS CAME and she was home for two weeks of laughter, snowballs and caroling. We walked beneath leaden skies and she recited lines she had learned from plays. We had a quiet but passionate Christmas Day at my condominium in town, then I was alone again with my routines. During the next three months, I received emails and letters. She had landed the role of Nora in *A Doll's House*. I meant to fly up during its two-week run, but an old client had shot her husband dead in their living room, so it was quite out of the question. Besides, Loretta would be home soon, I reasoned. I would see her then.

Spring break arrived and I picked her up at the airport. She had changed so much that she was embracing me before I knew who she was. Her hair was close-cropped and she had dyed it black—for a part, she said. She wore eyeliner, black tights, black skirt and an off-the-shoulder emerald green sweater that sharpened the green of her eyes to a piercing brilliance. She snuggled close like a new lover as we drove through town, and when we made love it was like having both her and a strange and exotic woman at once. Later we walked downtown and she sang "Good Morning Starshine" and "Don't Cry for Me Argentina." We rambled through a park, past lilacs and dogwoods. After all her songs, she would look to me for a judgment.

"Miss Garner," I would say, "You know I'm tone-deaf."

"How could I forget, Counselor?"

We went down Front Street, along the river to Club Manhattan, where my lawyer friends socialized, then stopped at Annie's Espresso

Cafe and watched students and businessmen stroll by. Loretta ordered to-go cups then led me outside, exulting in the exquisite levity of freedom. Every window was occasion for enthusiastic assessments of the trinkets displayed—each blossom on roadside trees an opportunity to sniff the fragrance.

"How will you ever adjust?" I asked as she tossed pennies in a fountain.

"Huh?" She looked at me, unblinking, her outlined eyes wide and black as kewpie dolls' beneath her black hair, against her white skin.

I said the obvious as gently as I could. "This isn't going to last forever, you know." She didn't answer. "Have you been by the paper at all?" She looked away. "Let's go see your old friends," I suggested. "It'll ease the transition." She nodded, but when we got to the front steps of *The News-Pulse,* she stopped. Slowly she looked inside, past her own reflection there in the plate glass windows. She took in all the tired, graying forms bent over keyboards. Former colleagues looked at her as if watching a curiosity, and one or two male reporters raised eyebrows flirtatiously, but recognition never dawned.

"I can't go in there," she said.

❧

Loretta's nine months would be up soon, she reminded me as I took her to the airport, but she never got around to telling me when they would end. In fact, she began to hedge when I'd ask by phone or email. Not that I was worried. One day the phone would ring to reveal a despairing voice, and I was prepared to be magnanimous, gallant even. I bought fine perfume for her as consolation.

I was made aware that her fellowship had ended as I sipped scotch one evening while studying legal briefs at a picnic table on my deck. It was the last day of May, with spring in full flower. I was feeling the first warm blush from my drink, and was about to put away my papers and savor the evening undisturbed, when the phone rang. I picked up the cordless receiver beside me and heard the dry rattle of keyboards in the background. I figured correctly that it was Loretta's editor.

Jules was direct, as always. "Have you seen Loretta?"

"Not since spring break," I said.

He sounded insulted, almost hurt, when he spoke again. "Do you know how to reach her?"

It occurred to me that she'd never promised to return on any particular date. Then I realized with a start that she'd never promised to come back at all—a point I'd ignored the whole time she was away. I felt blood drain from my face.

"Hello?"

"I - I can give you her number in Ann Arbor," I managed to articulate.

"I've tried there. Her landlady said school's been out three weeks, but Loretta didn't leave a forwarding address. I thought you might've been in touch."

"She called two days ago," I said. I realized she'd been the one to make all the calls recently—increasingly brief, breathless calls, especially the last several. There had been no emails or letters in weeks. "Strange," was all I could say.

"Strange isn't the word for it," Jules said. "Hell, I'm holding a slot for her. I let the temp go two weeks back. You don't think she would have *stiffed* us, do you?"

I remembered telling her to ignore the pledge to return and I felt myself blush. "Loretta is a dependable person." Even as I said it, I realized how little I knew this mercurial woman whose beauty had graced my life these last two years.

"Yeah, well, thanks for nothing," Jules said and hung up. I stood abruptly, knocking a file from my table, and watched fascinated as papers scattered in the breeze. My hand was trembling when I picked up the phone again and began dialing numbers with the sensation I'd known once when a case turned unexpectedly sour. It's devastating when that happens. Afterward, you lie awake at night considering every motion, every objection, every phone call not made, every false start. You try to compensate.

I spoke with a landlady who was angry because Loretta had given no notice when she left. And a drama professor who spoke highly of her *"joie de vivre,"* her "talent for inflection and innate stagecraft." I spoke with Loretta's mother, a country matron from the mountains fifty miles southeast of Lexington. She began sniffling at mention of Loretta's name and begged me to phone if I heard anything. There was a trace of Loretta in her voice, and I envisioned a freckle-faced, red-haired little girl spinning round and round on a tire swing suspended from a tree. Loretta had come a long ways.

Jules phoned several times during the next week but neither of us had news. He stopped calling one day, and a new byline began appearing above all those features in *The News-Pulse,* but the features lacked verve.

◈

LORETTA'S LAST LETTER arrived this morning, July 5. The envelope bore a New York return address. Inside was a smaller package. I knew as I unwrapped it that it contained the diamond ring. She had scrawled on a small piece of lavender stationery seven simple words, *"You didn't even listen to my lines."* Remorse seized me by the throat. I'd never read a more succinct indictment.

Something gray and insubstantial slipped from the envelope and fluttered toward the ground. The wind picked it up and carried it into the front lawn of the condo, and I pursued it among the rhododendrons bordering the walkway, catching it before it surely would have been swept into the streets.

My fingers fumbled with the scrap of newsprint. I held it in the morning sunlight and saw that it was from *The Village Voice.* It described an off-off Broadway play entitled *Vagabond Neon-Heart.* It was a moment before I realized what the clipping portended, but when I did, the wonder of it made me smile. Following the word "Cast" was a list of names, and fourth from the end was...*Loretta Dupree.*

I stood there a long time waiting to discover which of my warring emotions would prevail in the empty courtroom of my mind. For the moment my smile held sway. There is, after all, a kind of satisfaction to be had in recognizing how dead wrong you can be. It confirms old assessments of one's basic banality, reaffirms the part of you that wondered all along who the hell you were trying to fool. I whispered to myself, *I could've told you this would happen.* Then, unaccountably, I felt tears fill my eyes. Only for a moment, you understand, then I went upstairs and called the New York theatre named in the notice and made a reservation for this evening's performance. I was able to claim the last seat.

177

Sitting here at Gate Seven, I realize it may be too late to win Loretta back, but I'm going to pay her the attention she deserves. I will look intently from the front row and listen closely to all of her lines. I will assess every nuance of her performance. It's way time I took the measure of this phenomenon who calls herself Dupree. I have been indicted for a crime that carries a mandatory penalty—a lifetime of loneliness and regret. I must make my defense.◆

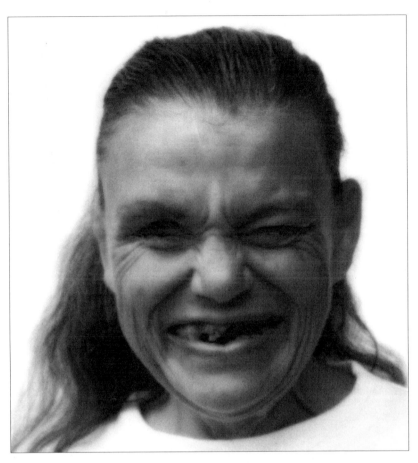

JUNE
by David Habercom

THE WELL
by Bob R. Wilson

The Metaphors

Jo Angela Edwins

COMMEMORATION

On the eighth anniversary
of the last day my mother was alive,
Columbia shattered on re-entry.
TV anchormen in crisp, dark suits
spoke in dulled voices,
groped for explanations,
interviewed professors,
insisted they knew nothing official,
and mispronounced the astronauts' names.

By late afternoon we'd seen pictures
dozens of times, the ice-white trail slicing
through a baby-blue sky, dark metal twisted
like a modern sculpture imbedded in the center
of some small town square, as if the citizens
sanctified the site for their own fallen children.
They were warned not to touch what they saw.

That afternoon my sister,
seventeen years older, called
from three hundred miles away.
We were nearer each other
than we were the disaster, but she
needed someone to talk to then,
and I suppose I did too. Both of us
unmarried, overweight, overeducated,
we knew without saying that what we feared

was our own lonely deaths, the mystery that scared us
that moment into buzzing silences.
In her new house back home she sat,
surrounded by boxes, listening to the television
droning in the other room.
"Those poor families," she said,
her voice as tired
as the thin winter sunlight
spilling through a sheered window
onto the back of my neck.
At first I said nothing. Then I remembered
a sad story we shared:
the time two springs before when I stepped
out to my car and found underneath it
a thin, silver cat, yowling as if
I were his mother. I lured him out,
patted his head, tickled his chin,
told him I wished I could keep him to myself,
but already I had one more cat
than the building allowed. My sister wondered
why I didn't at least feed him
a bowl of milk, a can of tuna,
something. I couldn't answer.
"You're cruel," she had giggled. Retelling
the story, I giggled myself, but she
said nothing this time. "I don't know why
I reminded you of that," I said.
"Me, neither," she said. "Come home," she said.
Then nothing.
                    Until
we spoke our small goodbyes. The phone line
crackled, and the TV showed again
sky burning vivid as superheroes,
next only to God,
too strong and too distant
for dazed, hungry people to touch.

Andrew Kleczek

PERISTALSIS

Standing over the toilet, I hear mother's scream. The boiler-that-is-my-father heats up. Steam's building. Suddenly, she's here. A cabinet drawer halts the door that I painted yellow at age twelve. Grabbing the scripted brown bottle and a baptismal hand of water, she swallows. Numbered globes spin out, dropping in: a countdown. Peristalsis (or is it paralysis?) wills them on. *Don't worry honey,* she says, slumped against the wall. *The world rests on a turtle, and it's turtles, turtles, turtles all the way down.*

Kelley Jean White

1971

Billy Starr suggested Purple Haze
and that might have been a kinder
act: prom couples staggering
in and out of violet mist and grinding
guitar riffs. But no one knew for sure
how to do the color effect
and concerns were raised
over safety and expense—
truth be told, nobody wanted to spend
a fortune on a gown and disappear—
so, Carousel. Which meant
all the girls in the Queen's court got
a fancy painted cardboard horse
to keep forever on their bedroom walls
and we had another reason to borrow
the green grass carpet from Mr. Gray
at the funeral home.

La Plaza de Toros de Sevilla, Spain
by Pamela Schoenewaldt

Patricia Waters

erro, errare
means i wander, to wander

There is no arriving,
only going
till a stop,
empty tank,
empty stomach,
full bladder,
tired body,
a stop all too brief
till the getting up,
filmy matter in the eyes,
half-remembered dreams,
shower, coffee, then the road again,
day's going, a careful watching.
There is the conversation with the radio,
news of financial markets,
disappearing species of flowering plants,
never-ending tournaments,
ludic emptiness,
and music of such beauty
that you must stop and weep
because you do remember
what came before the road
when you were still yourself.

Ana Anderson

RICE AND BEANS

Some Saturday afternoons I spent inside the kitchen,
accidental apprentice to my mother's *feijoada*.
I hung my brown legs over the counter, scabs on both knees,
badges of initiation, proof that my skin
was sturdy enough to live in the same world as my brothers.
I watched as she sliced onions, washed beans,
boiled rice, attended all the while
by the measures of Puccini
that floated from the turntable in the den.
She should have gripped my face between calloused hands,
pointed the knife at the stove and said *Look.*
This is important, this is what we have always kept.
Instead I trained my thoughts on the grass outside,
wondered what possessed Butterfly to swallow
her father's knife for a man with a name like Pinkerton.
I'm not sure what it is then that drives me years later
to curve my own cramped neck over the churning beans,
trying to translate from the ciphers
of memory the recipe she knew like language,
choking out my own aria of apology.

DOWN THE RABBIT HOLE

"We're all mad here," said the Cheshire Cat. "I'm mad, you're mad."
"How do you know I'm mad?" said Alice.
"You must be," said the Cat, "or you wouldn't have come here."

When Alice fell down the rabbit-hole and, later, when she walked through the looking-glass, she found herself in dream worlds that contained metamorphic pieces of her waking life, connections that were familiar yet alien in form and substance—chess pieces that came to life, the red queen in her arms transformed into one of her kittens. In dreams everything that should-n't happen *does* happen. We dream that we kill ourselves and then worry about where we will hide the body. We lose our babies and later discover them in the refrigerator. We make love with complete strangers, or, sometimes, the husband of a friend, and wake feeling guilty. We levitate, unsurprised that we float on mere vapors of air.

No reservations can be booked for the kinds of travel or the places where our dreams take us. In the human mind there are more continents and rivers and oceans, more longitudes, latitudes and solar systems than could ever be imagined here on this planet. Even on a real, earthbound journey, some events are dreamlike—seeing, in a Paris Metro station, a begging gypsy woman, her arms jangling with gold bracelets, imploring strangers to give her a few francs for milk while her baby sleeps against her breast. Where does she live? Is the baby drugged? Is there a husband who loves her?

Or there is the figure painted gold, standing on a street corner in New York, an unblinking sphinx, utterly immovable in the midst of traffic and pedestrian chaos. Who dresses this person every day? Who paints her? Or him? When does she eat, and where?

Many of my actual travels have seemed dreamlike as well. Years ago, I walked on the rocky beaches of the French Riviera, where the sea air smelled like old money, walked past achingly thin women who posed, just so, wrists dangling over the arms of their brightly colored sling chairs, faces and breasts exposed to the sun. At the shoreline old men stood, wearing gold neck chains and red silk thongs, tanned to leather by the Mediterranean sun and squinting out over the limpid waves, blowing blue smoke from their Gauloises and searching for some unnameable yet irreplaceable thing they seem to have lost.

One morning, at a news stand on the *Rue de Rivoli*, headlines screamed from newspapers ruffled by the cool ocean breeze: *"Marilyn est morte!"* People were weeping. Like Americans, the French were besotted with Marilyn Monroe. Was it because, like many of their own women, she wore no underwear? Or was it her *joie de vivre*, the last remnants of which she had quenched with the handful of pills the night before? It seemed to me as if, by being away from home in her worst hour, I had somehow failed her.

Years later, on another journey, I stared into the cavernous mouth of the Grand Canyon in the late afternoon when the shadows of its ancient yaw blended with the colors of the sky—azure, indigo and burnt sienna. Instead of marveling over God's great creation, I thought of those who have been seduced by the canyon's irresistible gravitational allure, have spread their empty arms and stepped off into the wide, vaporous air. I didn't want to think about their last moments. I wanted only to imagine the weightless elegance of their descent, the romance of it, the drama, the unbearable beauty of their unquenchable pain.

I remember other dreamlike journeys: Paris, where my second daughter was born; Barcelona, where I ate the best meal of my life, a dish of mussels in a red wine sauce; Ibeza, and the trip where I slept on the deck of a ferryboat under a canopy of a million stars; Florence, where I felt like a character in *Light in the Piazza*; Normandy, where, weeping as I walked on the beaches bloodied on D-Day, I found a heart-shaped granite stone carved by centuries of tides and imagined it as the petrified remnant of one of the brave young soldiers who had died there; the Baths of Caracalla, where I watched an evening outdoor performance of *Aida*, replete with real live elephants and camels.

But the most haunting and terrifying journey I have ever taken was one I cannot even remember, will never be able to recall. What I know of it comes only through the stories of those who witnessed it, and what I remember is only an inexplicable void that lasted for seven hours.

It had been a difficult year—death of a former spouse, family divorce, illness, bitter disappointments and failed communications. On a sunny morning, cool for August, I decided to take advantage of the shade in the backyard to work in my garden. We had just returned from Virginia, where we had visited my mother. She had suffered a series of small but debilitating strokes. When we left, she was recovering and in good spirits, but the visit had been stressful. It was the closest we had ever come to losing her.

I remember the sun rising higher that day, pushing itself into the corners of the garden. Enervating heat followed. Only a little while, I remember thinking, and I will be finished. I remember the glass of water I drank from, a tall clear glass decorated with orange goldfish that seemed to be swimming inside it. I remember laying down my rake and sitting on the steps for a few minutes, admiring the neat appearance of my flower beds. A large pile of grass and weeds lay on the pea gravel as evidence of my labor. I remember going inside the house and climbing the stairs, then turning on the shower and feeling dizzy and violently ill, vomiting. That's when I stepped into the rabbit hole. That's when I lost seven hours of my life that can never be recovered.

∽◌◠

"I wonder if I shall fall right through the earth!"

∽◌◠

WHEN MY FAMILY TELLS ME what happened to me on that strange, dreamlike day, my heart knocks against my chest. I feel like crying. I hyperventilate. Because I don't know that person they saw the day I stepped into the rabbit hole. It's as if she's a strange, frightening woman they have invented, but no. It happened. There are hospital records to prove it. There are follow-up visits to confirm it, insurance records, bills, and, for a few weeks, there was the proof of their worry as my children and husband watched me more closely, and asked me, too often, how I felt.

The day it happened, I called my son. I was crying. "I'm sick," I told him, and then asked the questions I was to repeat hundreds of times that day: "What's wrong? What's happening?" And then, synchronicity. Just minutes later, my husband called home just to say hello, and I asked the same questions. "What's happening? What's the matter?" Both of them rushed to the house and found me in bed in my nightgown, my hair wet from the shower.

∽◎∾

"Your hair wants cutting," said the Hatter. He had been looking at Alice for some time with great curiosity.

"You should learn not to make personal remarks," Alice said with some severity: "It's very rude."

∽◎∾

ADDRESSING MY CONSTANT QUESTIONING with the constant reply, "I don't know," my husband managed to get me dressed and into the car. I don't remember his speeding to the hospital, but he tells me now that I screamed as he leaned on the horn and veered around the impeding traffic. I joke and tell him that is not unusual, that I often scream when he drives, but I remember nothing of that terrifying trip to the emergency room. Everything else that happened that day is also second-hand information. My son and daughters arrived at the hospital and watched helplessly as I lay on a gurney, weeping inconsolably and asking the ubiquitous question: "What's happening?"

Sunstroke was the initial diagnosis of the handsome young East Indian doctor who treated me that day, but after a few tests, he changed his mind. He was kind and patient, and extremely puzzled. No signs of dehydration, he told my husband, and no evidence of a cerebral incident.

After I was given a sedative and had calmed down a little, I correctly answered all the doctor's questions: What were the names and birth dates of my children? Who was the president? What day was it? I counted, at his request, backwards from one hundred in increments of seven. All this without a single mistake. No mental damage. And aside from complaints about feeling a pressure on my legs, no adverse physical effects. Still I continued to ask the omnipresent question: "What's happening?"

A series of tests followed—MRI, CAT scan, EEG, EKG, x-rays. No adverse indications. And then, at about 6 p.m., something suddenly turned back on in my brain. I came up from the rabbit hole. It was as if I had been deaf, dumb and blind for most of the day, and now I suddenly found myself on a gurney, looking up at the worried faces of my husband and my three adult children. The eeriest thing about my awakening was that I felt no surprise at being there, in those circumstances, and now that "What's happening?" would have been an appropriate question, it didn't occur to me to utter it.

⊷⊶

"Everything's got a moral, if only you can find it."

⊷⊶

SLOWLY, AFTER I WAS WHEELED to a room and my situation gradually revealed itself, the enormity of my predicament began to dawn on me. As yet, there was no answer as to what my diagnosis might be, no name for the episode I had experienced. The next morning the doctor came into my room, smiled, tweaked my blanketed toe, and said that all tests showed nothing wrong. I was fine, he said. I could go home. But there were still many unanswered questions. What, exactly, had happened? Was there a name for it? Would it happen again? What was the long-term prognosis? My lovely, long-lashed and sympathetic doctor instructed me to visit my regular internist for a follow-up and released me from the hospital. I was frightened, terrified of the slightest physical tic or flutter in my body. I was afraid to drive, afraid to venture out into the August heat. I stayed close to home, worried that the mysterious condition might suddenly overtake me again.

But the next week, my internist, a brilliant physician and epidemiologist, had the answer as soon as I described the first symptoms. Transient global amnesia (TGA), technically caused by deactivation of the mesial temporal lobes and/or thalamus and triggered by external stresses such as emotional events, strenuous exertion, sexual intercourse, or immersion in extremely cold water. Simply put, TGA closes down the part of the brain that controls short-term memory. Perhaps this is to give the emotionally stressed victim a break from worrying, a small vacation from everyday life. Despite this partial shut-down, the patient can remember anything learned before the event, even efficiently drive a car or perform any chore while experiencing the symptoms, but during the average one to eight hours of the event itself, nothing is retained by the brain, nothing sticks, including the answer to "What's happening?"

Symptoms are limited to temporary amnesia, with no aphasia (loss of power to utter or understand words) or apraxia (physical damage or paralysis). While the patient experiences the episode, she is disoriented about time and place, exhibits repetitive questioning ("What's happening?") and can follow complex commands ("Count backwards from 100 by increments of seven") and does not confabulate (fill in the gaps with fictitious information). And the best news is that, in general, transient global amnesia rarely recurs. "True TGA," says the medical information, "has a benign prognosis."

After my internist's optimistic explanation and my promise to return for a follow-up in a month, I fairly floated out of his office, drove home without trepidation, and called everyone who knew I had suffered this strange malady. I had climbed out of the rabbit hole, walked back through the looking glass, awakened from a nightmare I couldn't even recall. For a week or so, I tested myself: Did I remember things I had done five minutes before, an hour before? I reviewed the day's events to confirm my mental condition. This happened last summer, and my memory remains intact except for when I misplace my glasses or car keys or forget the name of an old acquaintance. (Statistics say that after the age of forty, the average person forgets the names of two-thirds of her former friends.)

Will I ever be able to retrieve those mysterious seven hours? No, and

I feel cheated. I love my life too much to have lost so much time, and yet, who knows what my subconscious might have stored during that unusual journey? Something that will eventually evolve through one of my stories? Jabberwocky? Perhaps, but isn't every language invented anyway? Just as our dreams are invented by the very lives we live. To reclaim those lost hours, or to discover just what I learned during that dark episode—that's a journey I also look forward to, a dream as yet undreamed, but highly anticipated.

◦❀◦

"It was much pleasanter at home," said Alice. "And yet, and yet—it's rather curious, you know, this sort of life." ◆

Deborah Scaperoth

PHILOLOGY:
ONE WOMAN'S ODYSSEY

In the beginning was the word
and the first beloved word was errant
at least as spoken by a neighbor
on the phone: "Is my errant son there?"
Errant. I liked its sound and vowed
to use it in casual talk:
"Has my errant letter arrived yet?"
"Please excuse my errant behavior!"

Errant then defined me.
In high school, I forged
my mother's signature
to skip class and took the train
into Chicago for high adventure.
I dragged my younger sister with me
and we tied love knots
in our long, shining hair.

Then the wild years came
and the words became flesh
as I sought salacious,
sybaritic, peripatetic.
Then one night I found myself
singing lullabies to three small children
who didn't know the word errant
and it was enough.

I sang the same words
from the same songs for years.
Now, I'm in love with new words,
but unlike the aging sailor who vowed
to seek knowledge like a sinking star,
I want to seal my ears with wax
because I'm too tired to chase
the wildest ones again.

My son, the half-marathon runner,
says the secret to winning races
is not to get lost in words or thoughts
when running, but to focus
on moving forward, the next step.
His words shine like lights.

Doris Ivie

THE TWENTY-SEVENTH WINTER

For twenty-seven years they have weathered
the accusations, the name-calling, the fights. But
now the boys are grown, their glue has cracked,
their furniture is falling apart. Now in this three-
cubed year when they bother to look into
each other's eyes there is no light. He spends
more time in town, she orders more cable channels.
She throws herself into her work, he halves his.
He begins to write poetry, she explodes.
She tells him to get out of her life, he retreats.
From all appearances they seem to have resolved
their differences, for he no longer cares,
no longer bothers to retort. They're hanging there
like so much frozen laundry, but this time
there'll be no spring thaw. He's packing his clothes,
selling his books, counting his coins, planning his escape—
and really, she tells herself, she could care less.

Jane Hicks

CHRONOLOGY OF A DREAMER

Lee Smith: "What would you do if somebody
told you that you weren't allowed to write anymore?"
Lou Crabtree: "Well, I reckon I'd just have to sneak
off and do it."

Woolgathering, mama called it.
Get that wash out, quit staring
at them hills. I'd sneak and do it
through the galluses of the overalls
and flapping feed sack sheets.
Stuck a book in my bucket those
hot berry-picking days. I'd read
it on the far side of a briar patch,
on hot huckleberry mountains.

Mooney-eyed my man called it.
Where's my cornbread, been staring
at them hills all day? That baby's
just spoiled ... quit petting it so.
Stuck a book in my basket those
herb-picking days on the ridge.
Wildflowers marked the small
stones of short lives. The man
wandered off to another holler
to daddy a passel of farm hands.

Bookish, the others called it,
keeping school for children

I couldn't have, the writing of my sly self
became my letter to the world—
how a bookish woman saved her soul—
standing waist-deep in the hard life,
the books brought me to shore.

Rough hands tender my book
to me. I sign it to a sister
and know if I couldn't write,
I'd have to sneak and do it, she'd
have to sneak and read it,
our souls roam the dark hills.

DESCENT, CHARLESTON
by Nick DeFord

Life Among the Lilliputians

*F*or most of my youth, I felt like Mrs. Gulliver living among the Lilliputians. A head taller than my friends, my older brother, and even many of my teachers, I did not appreciate my long-limbed body. The tallest girl, the tallest person, and the tallest object in the classroom, I felt like a skyscraper.

Lofting me to this height was a pair of spidery long legs with knobby knees and skinny ankles, accompanied by feet the size of boat oars. I longed to be dainty and petite like my girlfriends who batted their eyelashes as they looked up at boys faces. I never looked *up* at boys. I looked *down* upon their dandruff-ridden heads.

Instead of 'gorgeous' or 'good-looking,' my nicknames included 'Wilt the Stilt,' 'Beanpole,' and 'Long Tall Sally.' Thankfully, I learned to laugh at myself early in life, and my sense of humor enabled me to deflect the insensitive comments I heard.

I'll never forget my first dance in junior high, which I looked forward to with great anticipation. In preparation for the event, we practiced the mambo, the cha cha, and the jitterbug in gym class. Though my feet were big, I could float like a butterfly on the dance floor. Unfortunately, none of the dwarf boys at the dance invited me to flutter from my cocoon. "Cherry-Pink and Apple-Blossom White" echoed from the record player as I languished on the sidelines, watching the midget boys dance with the short girls while the Amazons like me wallowed in envy and boredom.

When I lamented my height to my mother, she confessed that she, too, had dreamed of being shorter when she was a young girl. She tried to solve the problem in a unique way by asking to sleep with her sister Ellis, who at five feet, three inches tall was the shortest of Mom's five sisters. Somehow, Mother reasoned that sleeping with Ellis would magically stunt her growth. Of course, her strategy failed. Mother ended up being the tallest sister of all at five feet, nine inches.

By the age of thirteen, I had surpassed Mother's height and sprouted up like a sunflower to five feet, ten inches. My attempts to appear shorter by wearing low-heeled shoes and a flat hairdo did not succeed, though I hunched my shoulders forward and bent my knees as much as I could. During every class photo or chorus concert, I stood on the back row. If someone moved me to another row temporarily, there was an immediate outcry of "I can't see over Judy."

In high school, the situation improved slightly since some of the boys grew a few inches. However, I still stood out in a crowd of girls like a scarecrow in a tomato patch. My height wasn't quite the disadvantage it had been though. When I auditioned successfully for the school's modern dance group, my angular arms and legs fit in perfectly, and the judges raved over my high leaps into the air.

In college, I began to appreciate my height. Suddenly, being tall was an advantage, especially if you played sports. Selected for the varsity basketball team, volleyball team, and swimming team, I out-jumped and out-spiked my opponents, and my elongated body was a definite asset when I competed in the butterfly stroke.

My good fortune continued. Cast as Maggie, the funeral dancer, in *Brigadoon*, my stature allowed me to perform dramatic arabesques and poses quite suitable to the role. Other dancing roles followed in *Carousel* and *The Boyfriend*. On stage, not a single person asked me "how's the weather up there?"

At last, others viewed me as queenly and statuesque. A modeling agency hired me for part-time work, and even vertically challenged males eyed me from a different perspective. The ugly duckling had metamorphosed, maybe not into a swan but at least into a graceful ostrich. It was a great relief to leave the days behind when schoolmates laughed at my height.

Eventually, I married a good-looking Italian named Dan who was one inch shorter than I, but my height did not bother him at all. He didn't care if I wore sneakers, flats, or three-inch stiletto heels with sexy ankle straps. Of course, I didn't often wear stiletto heels for two reasons. First, I couldn't keep my balance in them, and, secondly, Dan might get tired of talking to my chest—or maybe not.

Infrequently, I still encounter ill-bred people who can't appreciate tall women. I treat their flawed outlook with disdain since I am far above their petty views, both literally and figuratively. However, sometimes one of my big feet accidentally sticks out and trips them.

I have traveled from stick girl to gawky teenager to mature woman. Although I am still taller than most of my friends, I no longer feel like Mrs. Gulliver. In fact, I feel quite comfortable with my height. I don't need a ladder to reach the highest shelf, and I can see over the crowd at any parade.

Yes, I have finally accepted who I am.

I am tall. ◆

Lynn Veach Sadler

THREADING STARS

Despite the leg I dragged,
I threaded my way through stars
whose fields of magnetism
bound all together save me.

At length I bowed before a blind yogi
in Benares (Kashi, the "City of Light"),
"where the Ganges bends" and one climbs
her ghats to be liberated from Karma.

Yogi Kabir Das was a descendant of Babur,
founder of the Mughal Empire,
and was, on his father's side,
descended from Tamerlane ("Timur the Lame")
and, on his mother's, from Genghis Khan.

The old gentleman lived in one small room
close to the Vishvanatha Temple.
"What will you have, Learned Miss?"
He asked it as I knocked and entered.
"I would first see if what I would have
is all right to seek."
He nodded as if pleased.
"I've wandered a wilderness of stars to you."
Again he nodded, then asked, "Why am I the one?"
"Because...in Somnath was the Siva lingam."
Why I'd said it, I didn't know,

205

but having had it rush out,
I remembered the great Somnath relic
floating, unsupported, in mid-air.
Another nod. Then, "Will you drink
from the cup and break it?"
I said "Yes" and was instantly gone.

I could see below me
women and some men (*dhobis*)
washing clothes in the Ganges,
barge loads of deodar and sweet-scented pine
floating down from the Himalayas.
I wondered if I could be seen
as what I was, a woman flying
on a geometrical figure of light.
Or was I perceived as satellite or comet
or some jettisoned piece
of space equipment gone mad?
My joyous laughter flowed behind me—
an arrangement on a musician's sketch pad.
The lost chord.
The music of the spheres.

When I was allowed to alight,
my still-dragging foot
no longer mattered so much.

If I Go Suddenly

A humid summer morning, plodding
        through a need-to walk,
I encountered other pilgrims chasing
health. One, a gray-haired senior,
walk more like a shuffle, leaning
to it like a horseman against
the wind, looked at risk of toppling
on the sidewalk, if not from heart
        attack, then bulging stomach,
full of no discipline.

        Audio apparatus wired
        to waist and earphones cuffed
        to feed his happy head with lifting
        music or maybe inspired words,
        his whole-face smile belied
        the facts. High blood pressure
        and arthritis could likely start
        the list. Still, he *good-morning'ed*

me with gusto. I walked my round,
the image taking hold, and sang
my song against the worried air.
        Back home, my mind embraced
the thought — *strolling a garden*
of green trees and God's bright
flowers, tuned to joy, leaning
into the future, smiling
at the world; a cheerful
        way to go.

Jerry Peterson

THE GIMP CLUB

$\mathcal{D}$octor Meadows lifted the gauze bandage that covered the stump. "Tell me, Rooster," he mused as he examined the stitches, "how'd you get that name of yours?"

"Don't know as you'd be much interested," his patient mumbled.

"Try me."

Rooster Wilhite, in a black mood for days, gazed away toward a window at the far end of the ward. The image there was blurred, but he forced himself to focus, not so much on the window itself, but on the frame, specifically on one corner of the frame, as if he were trying to figure out how the carpenters had cut the angles so precisely that the pieces fit together without any gaps.

I could never do that. Hell, I'll never do that, not with one arm, one hand...

"It's healing nicely," Meadows said. He put the end of his stethoscope on Rooster's chest. "I'll just check your heart."

He listened, then scribbled notes on a chart. "Not up to talking?"

"Huh-uh."

"Well, your heart's fine."

Rooster turned away. He rolled up on his good side and lost himself in the memory of a better time. A tear slipped from the corner of his eye.

Meadows gazed at his patient over the top of glasses riding low on his nose. He shook his head. The surgeon hung the chart on the end of the bed and silently left the ward, lost in his own thoughts, so lost that he walked into three of his former patients.

208

"Hey, you all right, Doc?" one asked.

"Just thinking."

"How's he doing?"

"Hmm?"

"Rooster. How's he doing?"

Meadows sighed, his hands thrust deep in the pockets of the white coat he never bothered to button. "In the dumps. It's hit him, all he's lost."

"He ready to see us?"

"Probably not, but make a go at him."

The three moved on into the ward, to bed number eight.

"Hey! Hey!" one called to the form that lay before them. He jabbed at the covers with his cane. One of the jabs caught Rooster in the middle of the back, inflicting such a sharp pain that Rooster wrenched himself around to find himself facing three grinning fools.

"Intending to sleep your life away?" the first fool asked.

"Come on, sun's up," said the second.

"We got places to go," chimed in the third.

"Then go!" Rooster bellowed. "Hell, I don't know you people."

"Oooo, he's testy," the second fool said to the third.

"Suppose we ought to tell this sorry excuse why we're here?" the third asked.

"Can't you see I'm hurtin'?" Rooster held out his empty sleeve. He shook it at them. "Leave me be!"

"Can't do that, bud," said the second.

"Why the hell not?"

"Because Doc Meadows sent us," said the third, a man, Rooster saw clearly now, who sat in a wheelchair. "You see, we're members of the doc's Gimp Club and so are you." The man whipped a blanket away from his lap. "No legs. Lost 'em in a slate fall—coal miner."

Number two held out his right arm. "Railcar coupling crushed my hand. Doc had to take it off—brakeman for the L&N."

Number one put his right leg up on Rooster's bed. He gave his leg a stout whack with his cane. "Solid wood. Got the real thing mangled at the White Lily flour mill."

"So now what the hell have you got to feel sorry about?" the wheelchair man asked, his eyes twinkling.

"Nothing!" his partners chorused. They did a doe-see-doe in the center of the ward, dancing over to Rooster. "Come on! We're taking you out of this sorry place."

The brakeman yanked the covers off the bed, and the flour miller pulled Rooster's legs around so he had to sit up.

"Where's your clothes?" "Gotta have clothes." "You still keep them in a box under the bed like we did ours?" Words tumbling out in bunches, roly-poly over one another.

The miller found the box with Rooster's boots. He pulled them out. Pairs of hands yanked Rooster into his britches, while one lone hand whipped his nightshirt off over his head and other hands stuffed him into a plaid shirt from the box—so many hands pushing, pulling, tucking and buttoning that objecting did no good.

The miller and the brakeman hauled Rooster to his feet. They stuffed him into his jacket. The brakeman placed Rooster's slouch hat on his arm and held it out. "Your hat, sir."

He took it, tentatively. Rooster didn't know what to do with it. He couldn't put it on because his mother had always told him to never wear a cap or a hat indoors, that gentlemen didn't do that. And he didn't know whether to be embarrassed or angry over being jerked out of bed by strangers and, worse, being undressed and dressed by them.

"Name's Fawcett," the man in the wheelchair said, holding out his hand. Rooster fumbled with his hat. He dropped it as he reached for the outstretched paw. The wheelchair man grinned. "Hiram Fawcett, but you can call me Leaky."

"I'm Edgar Wilhite..."

"It's Rooster, yeah, we know," said the man with the wooden leg. "I'm Albert Lee Brownlow. And this one-handed gent is Wil Buncombe, a dog of no particular pedigree."

Brownlow and Buncombe each put an arm around Rooster. They swept him out into the ward and toward the door that led to a world he had not seen for a month.

"We're taking you to dinner," Brownlow said as Fawcett rolled ahead of them.

Outside, the air had the crisp feel of autumn. The dogwoods and shagbark hickories that lined Clinch Avenue confirmed the change of season. The clustered berries of the dogwoods had turned a brilliant red, and the leaves of the shagbarks, a soft gold. When had that happened? Rooster wondered.

A jolting ride on the Red Line trolley deposited the quartet in the central business district. There they ambled on to Edna's Café.

Wil Buncombe, tall, gaunt, with a soup-strainer moustache prominent beneath his nose, read down the chalked menu on the blackboard in the front window. "What looks good to you?"

"Southern fried chicken," Rooster said.

"Snap beans? Fried okra? Mashed taters and gravy?"

"All of that. And hot biscuits, too."

"Soup? Gotta have soup," Leaky Fawcett said. He had been as lean as Buncombe when he worked a pick and shovel in the crawl spaces of the Black Diamond mine outside Oliver Springs. But Fawcett had filled out since the roof fall put him in a wheelchair. Shoulder and arm muscles bulged beneath his coat.

"Potato soup, gotta be potato soup," Rooster said.

"Like anything on the dessert menu?" Albert Lee Brownlow asked, the miller barrel-chested, arms thick as telephone poles.

"Sweet potato pie."

"Then we know what we're having for dinner. Rooster, get the door. We'll carry Leaky."

Brownlow and Buncombe each got hold of one side of Fawcett's wheelchair, Brownlow steadying the chair's back with his free hand. They swept the chair and its passenger up the steps and inside with the ease of someone carrying a bag of cotton.

Over soup and saltines, the three old members of the Gimp Club told the stories of their accidents. Rooster was amazed. These men laughed about what had happened to them and what had happened since.

"The first time I tried to tie my necktie with one hand, it was like trying to tie spaghetti!" Tears from laughter coursed down Buncombe's cheeks.

Albert Lee snorted. "Me? I've had an itch in my leg that won't quit. The first time my wife saw me scratching my wooden leg, she said, 'What's bothering you, termites?'"

"That's nothing," Leaky broke in. "The first time I tried to lift my-self out of my chair to get on the toilet, I fell flat on my butt. You should have seen me scrambling to get up, me with no legs. Musta looked like a hog on ice!"

Buncombe slapped the table and roared.

"I tell ya, it wasn't easy, and I said things I shouldn't have," Leaky rolled on, poking at Buncombe, "and all that time I had to go bad."

Rooster set his spoon aside. "So what did you do?"

"I went to the hardware store. I got me some pipes to attach to the walls for handles. Now it's nothing to get on the toilet. But Rooster, it's hell when I'm away from the house. So I always go with my wife or with friends like these, people who will help me."

Wilma, Edna's one and only waitress, brought out a monstrous plat-ter of fried chicken and put it in the center of the table. She cleared away the soup dishes, then brought out bowls of vegetables, gravy and a platter of hot biscuits. Rooster filled his plate so full he wished he had sideboards on it.

"What are you doing now?" he asked, glancing around at the men. "You can't still be shoveling coal or grinding flour or making up freight trains."

"Oh, I'm still at White Lily," Albert Lee said. "I'm still at the same job, but I'm damn careful not to stick my good leg in the machinery."

"Me?" Buncombe asked as he put away a chicken leg. "I'm a cop. Al-ways wanted to be. I was right-handed, but I can shoot a revolver with my left hand with the best of them."

"What about you, Leaky?" Rooster asked as he reached for a second helping of potatoes.

Fawcett put down the biscuit he'd buttered. "You're not going to be-lieve this, but I'm an apprentice tailor."

"The heck you say, a pick and shovel man?"

"Rooster, I can't do that no more. I don't have legs. There are a lot of things I can't do, but I got two hands, two good hands, two fast hands." Fawcett raised his hands. He wiggled his fingers. "I've been at it a year now and, damn, I'm good. You know what's the best part?"

Rooster couldn't speak with his mouth full of chicken.

"Now I don't come home at night all black and sooty from coal dust.

Every day my wife had to wash my clothes. Every night I had to scrub myself in a tub of hot water beside the kitchen stove. You don't know what it means to a man to be clean until you've worked in a coal mine."

Albert Lee pushed his plate aside. Then he leaned on his elbows. "So, Rooster, what you gonna do?"

Rooster looked up, startled. He chewed on his mouthful of snap beans, finally swallowing them. "Can't work in the sawmill no more, I know that."

"You sure?" Albert Lee asked.

"The work's like digging coal or milling wheat, takes two arms."

"Maybe there's a job at your mill for a man with one arm."

"The men I work for, they said they'd make a job for me, but, hell, that's charity, and us Wilhites, we don't take charity, not from nobody. We make our own way."

Albert Lee waved at Wilma. He motioned to the empty coffee cups. "So how are you going to make your own way?"

Rooster fell silent for a long time. Fawcett and Buncombe ate quietly. Brownlow blew on the scalding coffee in his freshly filled cup.

"I don't know," Rooster said, barely above a whisper. "It scares me."

"We were all scared. That's natural," Albert Lee said. He put a hand on Rooster's arm, giving it a reassuring squeeze. "We worked past it and you will, too. The doc tells me you're a pilot. Any good?"

"I came home from the war with no holes in me. What's that tell you?"

"Enough. There's a fella putting together a couple planes and pilots so he can bid on an airmail contract. You ought to talk to him."

"Flying a plane takes two hands."

"That's not what I hear."

"What do you know? Have you ever flown a plane?"

Buncombe interrupted. "Have you ever tried to be a cop with just one hand? Who are you to say you can't fly a plane with one hand? You never had to do it before. Well, now you do. I never had to be a one-handed cop, but now I am and I'm good at it, just like Albert Lee and Leaky are good at what they do. So don't flap your gums at us about not being able to do something. It won't get you no sympathy 'round this table."

"Rooster," Albert Lee said, putting a hand on Buncombe's arm, "that's hard talk from a man who rarely raises his voice, but Wil's right."

Tears welled up on the rims of Rooster's eyes. "Hell, I can't even tie my shoes."

"Have you tried?" Buncombe asked.

"Yes!"

"Then you need someone to teach you." The railroader-turned-policeman shoved his chair back. He stood and put a foot on the chair, then he pulled the knot loose on his lace until the ends dangled at the sides of his shoe. Next Buncombe deftly pulled the ends of the lace tight with the fingers of his lone hand. He worked one end around and over the other until he'd formed half of a square knot. Then Buncombe looped the ends of the lace, one loop over and one loop under. He tied them into a bow knot that he snugged with his thumb and middle finger.

"It took me a week to get it down, but, damn, if I can do it, you can do it."

Albert Lee rapped on the table. "Son, you've just had your first lesson on how to get along on your own. What do you want to do, keep feeling sorry for yourself or get back in the world?"

"Get back in the world."

"Good." Albert Lee turned toward the kitchen door where the waitress stood visiting with the cafe's owner and cook, Edna. "Wilma, we're ready for some sweet potato pie."

"Not before I go to the toilet," Fawcett said.

Albert Lee grinned at Rooster. "Your second lesson. You get to help Leaky."

Buncombe pushed his chair back a second time. "Come on, Rooster. It takes two of us."

Wilma waved the men back through the kitchen, pointing to a room set back in the corner.

Rooster opened the door. He looked in. "We can't get the chair in here."

"Rarely can," Leaky said. "Watch."

He undid his belt and unbuttoned the fly on his specially tailored pants, the legs lopped off and sewn shut to cover his stumps. "Now you and Wil are going to pick me up. You put your arm under my left shoulder, and he'll put his arm under my right, and you both just lift. When you get me in there, I'll tug off my pants and you set me down on the pot. When I'm done, help me back in my pants and get me out. Voila!"

"He makes it sound simple," Rooster said to Buncombe.

"You do it a couple times, and you and your partner, you work out a rhythm." The men bent down and got their arms under Fawcett's shoulders.

"Now when we've got him up," Buncombe said, "Rooster, you turn and go sideways through the door first and we'll follow. When we're all inside, we'll all turn together so our backs are to the toilet. Leaky drops his pants, and we back up and set him down. Ready?"

"All right."

"Lift."

Going into the toilet, Rooster stumbled on the door sill.

"Careful, careful, careful!" Fawcett hollered through his laughter. "I'm the one that gets hurt if you drop me, you gimps!"

They swung around, all facing the front of the toilet room. Fawcett tugged at his pants legs, and his pants fell to the floor. "Set me down."

Hardly had Buncombe and Rooster relieved themselves of their burden than Fawcett relieved himself of his. The toilet thundered.

Buncombe and Rooster leaped from the room. They slammed the toilet door shut, then whipped open Edna's back door to get to the fresh air. There Buncombe leaned against the door jamb, breathing deeply.

"That's the only bad thing about helping Leaky. When he lets go, it's just awful." ◆

Ana Anderson

AFTERNOON

Listen. You're sitting at the
kitchen table, trudging through
another afternoon of History homework,
a chapter on Westward Movement
sprawled out across the tablecloth.
You're in third grade, maybe fourth,
and your mother's at the counter
cutting carrots for dinner.
You're so absorbed
in a painting of a woman and baby
stumbling in the snow
that you don't look up until
you hear your mother cry out,
don't see the quick
slip of the blade,
only the stream of blood.
Seven stitches later
the one thing you cannot escape
is how she's only a heartbeat
surrounded by muscle and bone,
trails of veins,
skin like paper that crumbles,
rips, burns.

Barbara Crooker

In January, My Middle Daughter Leaves Home

The seasons open and close like a fist,
and now it's winter, season of bones.
One blue jay at the feeder, flicker of a gas jet.
The millennial odometer turns O O O.
There is no difference between horizon and hill,
white on white on white.
Driving down the turnpike, I listen to Verdi's *Requiem*,
the snow making its own white music;
all the lines slant downward.
Crows clot the woods with night.

Janet M. Lewis

A Gentle, Loving
Disconnect

When I was a child
and Mom would drive me home
through the darkening streets,
we'd play a game:
If a house was lit up, we'd say,
"They're awake!"
Seeing a dark house, we'd say,
"Sleepyheads! They're asleep!"

When I was mostly grown,
Dad was driving me home
through the darkened streets.
I told him my new hopes,
plans and worries.
Would he be surprised?
disappointed? pleased?
I awaited his response anxiously.
"Look," he said at last.
"Every time we pass that house,
there's a light on in the kitchen!"
The quiet lay gently between us.
"They must do nothing but eat,"
I added.

Andrew Kleczek

DIMINISHING RETURNS

You seem shorter somehow,
diminished. Perhaps it was the illusion
of heels, mini stilts for your ego. Or maybe
your back's become a haggard oblique, a hunch of
meek humility

Your hands: a plasticized doll's—
rigid, with nails the ironic red of
Raggedy Anne.

Now, you are small enough, you could
fold up and slide into your purse, lie
beside the lip gloss, breath mints. Perhaps
snuggle in between a pack of Kleenex.

You might ride the shag back of a buffalo—a
brown cow tick, grasping—as it
thunders across the Dakotan plains.

With that near miniscule form you might
scurry across my Fitzgerald novel and hide
in the punctuation or even the capitalization, as
I read in the morning sun.

And now, now you are the tiny, near toothless
gears of the sky-eyed, crevassed,
Swiss jeweler's watch that we saw in Bern—turning
ever so slowly to the days of the month.

SLIDESHOW

*T*he numbers 1578 are etched in white on the curb in front of the birchwood house that your parents purchased for less than what they pay today for cars. The lilac bush next to the front door emits a fragrant aroma second only to barbeque smoke and the tang of freshly poured blacktop. A thin, metal gate with spaces shaped like diamonds leads into the backyard, which is also fenced with the same criss-crossing pattern.

The black-eyed Susans are the flowers you like most; you collect the tiny, black seeds in your plastic sand-pail already filled with the poisonous berries plucked from the bushes lining the outer boundary of your yard. Maybe add some twigs, some sand from the sandbox at the base of the deck stairs, or clumps of dirt still damp from the morning dew for your potion's finishing touch. Voila! Scurry toward the swing set, the bucket swinging in your clammy grip, until you leave it balanced precariously on a grassy mound. Swing higher and higher, legs kicking against the emptiness around, and listen to the swing set creak.

Often on hot summer days you paint the deck with a thick, bristly brush dipped in a bucket full of water. Or, when it's colder, you build a snowman in the backyard with your longhaired mother when the girls across the street don't invite you to participate in constructing theirs. You think of this even when winter's the furthest thought from your mind, sometimes, don't you?

Walk up the cement stairs to the front door, graze the lilacs so their scent bursts in your nose, and open the door and enter. You find yourself standing on a landing with a staircase ascending directly in front of you and a staircase descending to the left of that. Both are carpeted beige and aren't much softer than turf. Still, you're barefoot as often as possible. A metal-door closet is located to your immediate right, but you don't need to open it because it holds scarves, mittens, and coats, and it's summer. Even though you love your puffy, down jacket, it's your father's caramel suede with cowboy fringe you always reach for first.

Tramp down the stairs. To the right are more closet doors, where, that one year, you found a bird's nest near the furnace, and next to that stands the garage door. To your left, the family room waits, dark and airy. This is where you watch some of your favorite movies: *Star Wars*, for the first time; *Beast Master*; *The Neverending Story*. Walk toward the rarely lit fireplace, and brush past the chair your father would recline in when smoking his pipe or belting out Frankie Valley's highest notes. Your dad smoked only in the wintertime, and at the same time he'd grow a beard. He was almost like a mountain man, then, except for those hobbies he's long discarded. You're still enchanted with your parents' stacks and stacks of albums shelved haphazardly in the wall unit—remember them playing the record player loudly on weekends? You were always intrigued yet somewhat frightened by the Rolling Stones' album cover that sported a pull-down zipper.

Leave the family room and make your way toward the playroom—your second room—containing your miniature kitchen set; Clip Clop, your rocking horse; and the Barbie collection you'd later give away, on a whim and to your mother's confusion, one spring weekend afternoon. There's the little table at which you read, draw and sneak nibbles of Play-Doh underneath the windows that frame the ground level of the backyard. From your position you can see the black-eyed Susans and the beginning of your swing set. You spend hours in here just waiting for time to pass.

◦◦◦

ACROSS THE HALL, the bathroom opposite the playroom's entrance is tiny and cramped. Your brother or yourself—you can't remember which, isn't that funny? —crapped out a penny in here, and were both amused by that at the time, though he probably doesn't remember now.

If instead of going downstairs you had gone upstairs, immediately in front would have been the kitchen and directly to the left the living room. If you turn left into the living room, a railing protects you on your left, and the piano you so learned to loathe squats menacingly on your right. You remember Argie, your tri-colored collie, trying to poke his snout through the wooden railings whenever someone stood in the foyer or knocked on the door. You have a feeling this is the approximate spot where he lodged his tooth in your forehead while you crawled around on the carpet, under your father's care. Whenever your dad recollects that story you can just tell how scared he was at the time, though you're not sure if it was because of the blood gushing from your wound or because your mother wasn't home and would think him negligent.

In the living room, there is a blue and green, map-like, crushed velvet couch your parents would give to an aunt and uncle years later, which you secretly wish you had yourself. During Christmas time you'd set up the tree next to the couch and railing and string all the ornaments and lights together. Your mother still saves all the special ornaments in dusty boxes stacked in the basement—your Sesame Street favorites, the handmade ones with barely legible names and dates, the ones passed down from family. Windows line the wall behind the couch and provide a partial view of the front yard. There must have been another couch or chair, but you can't remember.

Some things just never reveal themselves, no matter how hard you try.

Off to the left side in front of you, once you're sitting on the couch, is the small dining room filled with the furniture passed down to your mother from her great-grandmother. The dining set was never your mother's style, but she still has it in the house she and your father live in today. There are many drawers, and on select occasions you go through them and find new treasures—tarnished silver, musty tablecloths, empty wrappers of your father's hidden sweets.

An opening in the right wall of the dining room functions as another entrance to the kitchen. There's that round, dark wood table, and lots of plain looking cabinets. The walls are covered with some sort of mustard colored 70s inspired wallpaper. Your mother allows you to climb in the bottom cabinets and play with the pots and pans while she cooks. You do this in the musty dark, loudly, waiting for a snack: celery stalks slathered with creamy peanut butter and sprinkled with raisins, if you're lucky. A sliding glass door leads to the porch, where, as I said before, you paint for hours. Is there a swinging bench? You think so. And if there isn't, there should be.

Leave the kitchen from the front doorway, turn left and approach a bathroom shared by your brother, your parents, and yourself on the left, and your brother's room on the right. He has a low-to-the-ground racecar bed covered with stickers and a fort your parents let you climb into at the top of his closet. It's almost as much fun as the kitchen cabinets. Almost.

Further down the hall is your room, with prettily rose-patterned wallpaper you can't believe you once loved, and your white, canopied bed. You have a wall length mirror that's part of a set your parents would later give to another aunt and uncle, a painted, wooden head with yarn braids hanging on the back of your door holding all your barrettes and headbands, a green framed print designating this Tracy's Room, and your favorite books. Look out the window: you see the sparse yet manicured landscaping of your front yard; the street on which you'd later hit a bunny with your Camaro, yet not kill it; and a friend's house beyond.

Your parents' room is next to yours. You love their big bed and crawl in between them when feeling scared or vaguely lonely. They have windows on two sides of the room—one on the west side of the house and one looking into the backyard. The one on the side, when open, lets in smells (that don't yet appeal to you) of the Indian family's cooking from next door. A massive, overwhelming TV that you love to watch rests on the floor. This is the room you inhabit when home sick from school. One of your favorite days is spent in this bed: a shadowy, wind-filled day in autumn when you read a lot; snoop through the bedside drawers; watch Fraggle Rock, the Muppets and leaves like jewels spiraling against the gray; are comforted with soup; and feel the fall air heaving through the open windows. On the wall to the left is another entrance to the bathroom. It's still the same.

It takes you a while to learn how to ride a bike. You'd try, and then throw it down in anger every time you failed, your father chuckling behind you, but always urging you on. Or how about that one time you came home from dance class and found your mother trying to save your poor goldfish—Sam and Samantha—in the kitchen sink. Your brother had overfed them—by accident, of course—and, in your eyes, became their killer. But your anger was soon forgotten, for the next weekend, there you were, making forts in the family room with old blankets and chairs, your mother humming as she descended the stairs, carrying sandwiches on white paper plates for you both.

It's been a long time, hasn't it? Feel free to visit any time. Any time, at all. ◆

Donna Doyle

DOWN BY THE HONEY

I forget what I am looking for.
As soon as the clerk says *It's down by the honey*
I forget what I am looking for, go there anyway,
down by the honey, down by the honey,
drowned by the honey dripping
over my tongue, sweet
repetition of rhythm washing me,
walking me toward what I have forgotten,
slow like winter bees warmed by sun, bodies
forgetting flight, forgetting
like mine, wakened by words weaving
me around light leading to you
standing there, down by the honey,
surrounded by honey, hair, honey, your hair
color of rain-soaked dry pine needles,
smile taking me to Tupelo and back, slipping
around my waist, dripping
down my hips, thighs, backs of my knees sticky,
tingling amber like memories we will make
down there, drowned there,
by honey.

SMALL JOURNEY
by Ellen Agee

CONTRIBUTING WRITERS & ARTISTS

ELLEN AGEE is from Richmond, Virginia. She moved to Knoxville after transferring from Virginia Commonwealth University to the University of Tennessee. Her interests include art, writing, photography and working with children. Agee says, "I got into taking black and white photographs of children at play while teaching pre-school in West Knoxville. Parents love my work and are always asking me to take pictures at their children's birthday parties and other events." Agee's goals for the future include writing and illustrating a children's book and one day opening her own childcare center specializing in art, music and drama.

CAMILA ALMEIDA is a creative writing major at the University of Tennessee at Knoxville. She moved to the United States from Argentina in January, 1986 with her family. Almeida is the eldest of five children; Eugenia and Raul are her parents. Almeida took Marilyn Kallett's poetry writing class in the fall of 2003. She writes short fiction and poetry and is working on her first novel.

ANA ANDERSON majored in Literature and creative writing at the University of Tennessee. By the time this anthology gets published, she will hopefully be in graduate school, pursuing her doctorate in literature— but she's not yet sure where. Anderson won the 2003 Knickerbocker Prize for Poetry at UT. This is her first publication.

JULIE AUER is a lawyer by profession. However, she has published short fiction, essays, and, as mystery writer Julia Lieber, a novel called *There Came Two Angels*. She is a past president of the Knoxville Writers' Guild and contributed to the KWG anthologies *Breathing the Same Air* and *Literary Lunch*.

STEPHEN AUSHERMAN is the author of the award-winning novel, *Typical Pigs*, and a collection of travel stories, *Restless Tribes*. He lives in New Mexico.

justin.barrett lives in Salt Lake City, Utah with his wife and dog. He works as a chemist and has been writing for over a decade. His first book was published in 2003 by Bottle of Smoke Press and was nominated for a Pushcart Prize. He is the editor of the online poetry journal *remark* and has started a poetry press with two other poets called Hemispherical Press. His second book, *The Magnificent Seven*, was just released by 12 Gauge Press.

REBECCA K. BROOKS received her Master of Arts degree in English, specializing in creative writing, from the University of Tennessee. She is a native East Tennessean and has three children and one grandson. She lives in Oak Ridge and is working on a novel about the people who left the Oak Ridge valley in 1942 in order for the government to build The Manhattan Project. Brooks enjoys writing short stories and non-fiction essays about Appalachian life. Her short story, "Double Edge," will be published in the fall issue of *Hawai'i Review*.

BILL BROWN teaches at Peabody College of Vanderbilt University. He is the author of four collections of poems. He has been a Scholar in Poetry at the Bread Loaf Writers Conference, a Fellow at the Virginia Center for the Creative Arts, and a two-time recipient of Poetry Fellowships from the Tennessee Arts Commission. He lives in the hills of Robertson County with his wife, Suzanne, and their cat, Soliloquy.

JEANNETTE BROWN has a Master's degree in Urban Studies and a career in publicity and PR for theatre, dance and other arts groups. Her work has been published in the *Texas Observer*, *ArtSpace*, *Mother Earth*, *Suddenly IV*,

Bellevue Literary Review and other publications. She is the editor of *Literary Lunch* and on the board of *The Ensign Literary Review*.

BARBARA CROOKER has published twelve chapbooks; *Impressionism*, forthcoming from Grayson Books, is the latest. Her poems have appeared in a variety of literary journals and many anthologies. She has won the 2004 Grayson Books Chapbook Competition; the 2004 Pennsylvania Center for the Book Poster Competition; the 2003 Thomas Merton Poetry of the Sacred Prize judged by Stanley Kunitz; the 2003 "April Is the Cruelest Month" competition, sponsored by *Poets & Writers*; First Place in the ByLine Chapbook competition, 2001; First Prize in the *Karamu* poetry contest, 1997; First Prize in the *New Millenium Writings* Y2K poetry contest, 2000; Grand Prize in the Dancing Poetry Competition (San Francisco), 2000; three Pennsylvania Council on the Arts Fellowships in Literature; seventeen nominations for the Pushcart Prize; a nod for the Grammies in the Spoken Word Category, 1997; and nine residencies at the Virginia Center for the Creative Arts. She lives in rural northeastern Pennsylvania with her husband and son, who has autism, and travels to France whenever she can.

NICK DEFORD is a recent graduate of the University of Tennessee with a B.F.A. in Studio Art and minors in English and Art History. He has had poems and artwork published in the University of Tennessee Literary Magazine, *The Phoenix*, and *Logos*, a student publication at the University of Kent in Canterbury, England. He is very proud to be a native Knoxvillian.

MARK DEKAY is an architect and Associate Professor of Architecture at the University of Tennessee where he teaches and researches about ecological approaches to buildings and cities. He studied architecture at Tulane University and the University of Oregon. Before coming to Knoxville, he taught at Virginia Tech and Washington University in St. Louis. He is author of *Sun, Wind, and Light: Architectural Design Strategies*, a book to assist architects in designing buildings that heat, cool, power, and light themselves with site-based renewable energy. DeKay spent half of 2000 on a Fulbright appointment to India.

EMILY DEWHIRST led a changed life following a fateful bicycle trip through Europe in 1947. Since then, she has had a lifelong commitment to adventurous travel and to working with people the world over. Never content to do things the easy way, she has traveled with Danish friends to the Arctic Circle on the back of a motorcycle, ridden camels on week-long trips in the Rajahstani desert in India and struggled with the cold and lack of food in Kazakhstan. Her journeys to Tibet, China, Morocco, Egypt and other countries have only whetted her appetite. She continues to travel, this year returning to Central Asia and Turkey. Emily is a hand weaver and passionate about all that is ethnic art and culture. She lives over her gallery, Nomad, on Market Square in downtown Knoxville.

JUDY DIGREGORIO is an award-winning humor columnist from Oak Ridge, Tennessee, who is a YWCA Woman of Distinction in Arts and Culture and the First Place winner of the creative writing Contest for the 2003 Virginia Highlands Festival. Her work has appeared in *The Writer*, *The Army/Navy Times*, *New Millennium Writings*, *CC Motorcycle NewsMagazine*, *Literary Lunch*, *The Church Musician*, and other publications. Judy also writes a monthly humor column for *Senior Living*, a newspaper distributed in five counties. Her current projects include a nonfiction book and a humorous one-act play.

DONNA DOYLE was born south of the Tennessee River in Knoxville. Her most enlightening journey was her eight and a half year pilgrimage with her dog, Sydney.

EMILY DZIUBAN is the editor of this volume and a board member for the Knoxville Writers' Guild. She holds a B.A. in English from Winthrop University in South Carolina and a M.A. in English from the University of Tennessee, where she currently teaches composition and literature classes. She has won John C. Hodges awards for her writing, teaching and tutoring. The Guild's previous anthology, *Literary Lunch*, published her short story "Rendezvous, Neither First Nor Last."

JO ANGELA EDWINS was born in Augusta, Georgia, in 1970. She was educated at Augusta State University and the University of Tennessee, where she was a three-time first prize winner in the John C. Hodges Graduate creative writing Contest for Poetry and where she received a Ph.D. in English in 2001. Her poem "My Mother's Hands" appeared in the Spring 2004 issue of *CrossRoads: A Southern Culture Annual*. She is an assistant professor of English at Francis Marion University in Florence, South Carolina, where she teaches composition and creative writing.

KEITH FLYNN studied at Mars Hill College and the University of North Carolina at Asheville, winning the Sandburg Prize for Poetry in 1985. He is lyricist and lead singer for a nationally acclaimed rock band, The Crystal Zoo, which has produced three albums: *Swimming Through Lake Eerie* (1992), *Pouch* (1996), and *Nervous Splendor*, a spoken-word and music compilation forthcoming in 2004. His poetry has appeared in many journals around the world, including *The Colorado Review, Rattle, The Cuirt Journal* (Ireland), *Word and Witness: 100 Years of NC Poetry, Poetry Wales, Shenandoah,* and *Crazyhorse*. He has been awarded the ASCAP Emerging Songwriter Prize, the Paumanok Poetry Prize and received two Pushcart nominations. He has published three collections of his work: *The Talking Drum* (1991), *The Book of Monsters* (1994), and *The Lost Sea* (2000). Flynn is founder and managing editor of *The Asheville Poetry Review*.

MATT FORSYTHE teaches creative writing and wilderness literature at the University of Tennessee, Knoxville. When not hidden behind a stack of papers and a cup of coffee at Borders Books or The Golden Roast Café, he can be found wandering the creeks and ridges of Great Smoky Mountains.

SUSANNA GREENBERG teaches in Washington D.C. elementary schools and lives in the Columbia Heights neighborhood of the District. She is a graduate of Yale University and a native of Philadelphia.

BRIAN GRIFFIN holds an M.F.A. in creative writing from the University of Virginia. His fiction, poetry and essays have appeared in numerous literary magazines. His collection, *Sparkman in the Sky*, received the Mary McCarthy Prize for Short Fiction and was hailed by the *New York*

Times Book Review as "beyond promising." He is Director and co-founder of the Peter Taylor Prize for the Novel.

DAVID HABERCOM grew up in Alabama in the 1940s and 50s. He pursued photography from age fourteen until his mid-thirties. After twenty-five years he returned to photography at age sixty-one. The second part of his ongoing project, "Invisible City," consists of thirty documentary portraits of the homeless in Knoxville, Tennessee.

JANE HICKS is a native of East Tennessee and an award-winning poet and quilter. She won the 2003 James Still Poetry Prize of the Appalachian Writers Association. Jane's poetry and criticism have appeared widely in the southeast, notably in *Appalachian Heritage, Appalachian Journal, Wind, Sow's Ear,* and *Now & Then.* Her work also appeared in *Literary Lunch.* Jane serves on the board of directors of the Tennessee Writers Alliance. Her "literary quilts" illustrate the works of playwright Jo Carson and novelists Sharyn McCrumb and Silas House. The quilts have been on tour with all these authors and hung in a show in *Gallery 105* in Shepherdstown, West Virginia.

LISA HORSTMAN is a children's book author/illustrator and book designer from Knoxville. An Ohio native, she moved to Tennessee in 1988 to work as a designer for Whittle Communications. From 1995-2002 she was the art director for *Metro Pulse,* a weekly Knoxville publication. While creating children's books, Lisa also designs award-winning publications for the National Park Service, the Great Smoky Mountains Association, and others. She is the designer of this volume.

DORIS IVIE, psychology professor and former English department head at Pellissippi State, edited *Breathing the Same Air: An East Tennessee Anthology* and Frank Jamison's *Marginal Notes.* Her work has been anthologized in *Cumberland Avenue Revisited, Anthem to a Scruffy City, Literary Lunch, The Voice of Memory,* and *All Around Us: Poems from the Valley,* and has appeared in the periodicals *Bountiful Health* and *New Millennium Writings.* She was honored with the Scottish Society of Knoxville's 2003 Celtic Heritage Award for her poem "Musings on Iona." Doris is currently trying to resist the urge to compile and edit an anthology of post-beat/pre-hippie memoirs because "people need to know that the Sixties happened in Knoxville, too."

MARTIN JACK is an English exchange student from the University of Kent, in Canterbury where he majors in American literature. He has been published in the British small press and has also served as a co-editor for the University of Kent literary magazine *Logos*.

FRANK JAMISON'S first book of poems, *Marginal Notes*, was published in 2001. His poetry, essays and children's stories have won numerous prizes. His poems have recently appeared in *Appalachian Heritage* and *Poet Lore*. His poem "My Mind Wanders" won the 2004 Robert Burns Competition of the Knoxville Writers' Guild. He is on the board of the Tennessee Mountain Writers Conference, a member of the Knoxville Writers' Guild and the Tennessee Writers Alliance. He lives and writes in Roane County, Tennessee.

STACY JONES, a native of Southwest Tennessee, received degrees in English from the University of Memphis and The University of Tennessee, where she received a graduate poetry writing award and was a featured reader of original poems at several Knoxville area venues. Her graduate work culminated in a book of poems titled *Rivers of Urgent Breath*. A former member of the Knoxville Writers' Guild's Board of Directors, Jones taught composition and creative writing at UT Knoxville for five years and participated in various writing workshops and residencies, including a fellowship at the Hambidge Center for Arts and Sciences in Rabun Gap, Georgia, and the Appalachian Writers Workshop in Hindman, Kentucky. She writes a weekly column for *The Daily Corinthian* in Corinth, Mississippi and plans to pursue a Master of Fine Arts degree in English. She enjoys swaying to the blues, savoring Southern cuisine, venturing to exotic locales and exalting life at every turn.

DAVID E. JOYNER, artist and illustrator, is a retired member of the conceptual staff of the Tennessee Valley Authority's Architectural Design Branch. He started writing short stories at the age of sixty-five and refers to himself as "an old man but a young writer." His work has been published in *New Millennium Writings* and *Literary Lunch*.

MARILYN KALLET holds the Hodges Chair for Distinguished Teaching at the University of Tennessee. She is the author of nine books, including *How to Get Heat Without Fire* (poetry) and *One for Each Night: Chanukah Tales and Recipes*. With Judith Ortiz Cofer, she co-edited *Sleeping With One Eye Open: Women Writers and the Art of Survival* . Kallet has won the Tennessee Arts Commission Literary Fellowship in poetry and was named Outstanding Woman in the Arts by the Knoxville YWCA in 2000. She is the poetry editor for *New Millenium Writings*. Her next book of poems, *Lure*, is forthcoming in 2005 from BkMk Press.

ANDREW KLECZEK studied poetry under Rhoda Janzen and Jack Ridl at Hope College. Kleczek lives in a suburb of Boston where he works as a mental health counselor.

TERESA JOY KRAMER's poetry has appeared in *Cicada, Open 24 Hours* and the Woman Made Gallery's *Her Mark 2004 Datebook*. A former journalist, she has worked in Indiana, Texas, and Mexico City. She recently received her M.F.A. from Southern Illinois University Carbondale and continues to live alongside the Shawnee National Forest in Illinois with two teen-age daughters who are negotiating their approach to womanhood.

JANET M. LEWIS lives in Fallston, Maryland. She is married with five children and sixteen grandchildren. A painter for years, she started writing poetry a few years ago. Her poetry has been published in *The Harford Poet*, the *Manor Born*, and *Poetry Ink*. Two poems have been accepted for *Sundry*. She has won a second prize in a Walrus Press contest and an honorable mention from the Oregon State Poetry Association.

JUDY LOEST is a free-lance writer and poet living in Knoxville. Her work has appeared in *Now & Then, The Cortland Review, Literary Lunch*, and *France Magazine*. Her occasional commentaries appear in *Metro Pulse*. In 2004, Loest won the Fine Lines Poetry Contest co-sponsored by Olay Total Effects and the Poetry Society of America.

JEANNE MCDONALD has published a novel, *Water Dreams*, and is co-author of two nonfiction books written with her husband: *The Serpent Handlers* and *Growing Up Southern*. She has also published short fiction, reviews and articles in anthologies, magazines, newspapers and journals. She is a recipient of the Tennessee Arts Commission/Alex Haley Fiction Fellowship, a Washington Prize in Fiction for an Unpublished Novel, and National League of American Pen Women and National Writers' Association novel awards. Retired from an editorial position at the University of Tennessee, she lives and writes in Knoxville.

FLOSSIE MCNABB has lived in Knoxville for over fifty years. Her poetry has been published in several anthologies and she was the assistant editor of *Literary Lunch*.

KAY NEWTON, a Memphis transplant, flourishes in the heart of Knoxville, where she writes stories, poems, songs, plays and articles. Among the highest honors her writing has received is that of having been included in all the Knoxville Writers' Guild anthologies published so far (but not the book of the memoirs, since Kay's too young to write her memoirs). She hopes the anthologies will keep coming out and that her work will continue to be included.

JO ANN PANTANIZOPOULOS has made many journeys, both geographical and cultural, in her life. She has a sign hanging over her washing machine that reads: "I wasn't born in Tennessee, but I got here as fast as I could." After being raised in Roswell, New Mexico, living in Greece and Switzerland for eight years and acquiring two new languages, she eventually landed in Knoxville. She has published Greek lullaby translations in *Two Lines*, as well as several articles on young adult literature, poetry translation in the high school English class and word play in various state English journals. Her personal essay "The Cornbread Legacy" was published in *Breathing the Same Air* as well as "My Fortune" and "Chamomile: Tea of Choice for Gods and Newborn Babies" in *Literary Lunch*. Pantanizopoulos recently won an award of excellence for her poem "Sunday Afternoon" in the 2003 Terry Semple Memorial Poetry Contest. In addition to her job as an administrator for Pellissippi State Technical Community College, she maintains websites for the Knoxville Writers' Guild, Pellissippi, Celtic Cat Publishing, and others.

CHRISTINE PARKHURST currently lives in Knoxville with her husband, George, 12-year old daughter Katie, Norwegian Elkhound called Elke and several fish. She has also lived in California, Texas and Europe and has traveled in many countries. She loves her family, children, dogs, reading, music, traveling (especially by train) and going for long walks with friends. She has written two unpublished books of psychological fiction, had "smidgeons" published in *Private Eye*, *She*, and *The San Francisco Chronicle* and read her stories on San Francisco Public Radio. Having chosen to avoid writing for several years in favor of having a "normal" job and lifestyle, she has begun once more putting pen to paper, and it feels great.

MARGARET PENNYCOOK, a native of Great Britain and habitual traveler, has spent much of the past three years roaming East Tennessee, interviewing and writing about local artists and craft workers. During that time she also visited and published pieces about Italy and Scotland in *The Slippery Rock Gazette*, to which she contributes frequent feature articles. She has won awards for fiction, nonfiction and poetry, and is the recipient of the 2001 Sue Ellen Hudson Award for Excellence in Writing from the Tennessee Mountain Writer's Conference and the 2001 Woodland Award for Poetry from the Cookeville Creative Writers' Association. She lives in Oak Ridge, Tennessee.

JERRY PETERSON learned the craft of writing short stories from Wilma Dykeman and studied novels with Allen Wier while a graduate student at the University of Tennessee. Peterson now lives and writes in Wisconsin. He has three manuscripts currently making the rounds of publishers.

DEBRA A. POOLE was born in Calloway County in Western Kentucky, raised in Southeast Alabama and moved to East Tennessee at age twenty-eight. She is a graduate of the University of Tennessee College of

Law and specializes in charitable giving issues. The Tennessee Mountain Writers awarded her First Prize for Nonfiction in 2001. Although she and her husband, Ray Pierce, live in landlocked west Knoxville, most of her recent writing seems to feature water.

STEPHEN ROGER POWERS is a Ph.D. candidate in the creative writing program at the University of Wisconsin at Milwaukee. His poems have appeared or are forthcoming in *Yemassee*, *Smartish Pace*, *Margie* and the University of Iowa Press anthology *Red, White, & Blues: Poetic Vistas on the Promise of America*. He has completed a book of poetry about his pilgrimages to Dollywood and his fascination with Dolly Parton.

DEBORAH REED has worked as an Off-Broadway stage electrician, librarian in the world's largest library on beer, farmer, charm school instructor, snake handler, and, most recently, as creator of Wood Sorrel, one of the nation's first environmentally-friendly residential developments. Her first novel, *Friends of Chickens*, is making the rounds. She is allergic to wheat.

JACK RENTFRO, depending on who's asking, is a freelance writer/editor, farmer or layabout. A Cleveland, Tennessee native, he worked for various area newspapers following graduation from the University of Tennessee school of Journalism in 1981. His work has appeared in Knoxville Writers' Guild anthologies *Literary Lunch* and *Breathing the Same Air*. Rentfro combined his love of music, history and writing in *Cumberland Avenue Revisited: Four Decades of Music from Knoxville, Tennessee*, an anthology he conceived as a celebration of Knoxville's under-appreciated pop, folk and jazz music scenes.

KRISTIN ROBERTSON teaches creative writing at the University of Tennessee. She holds a B.A. and an M.A. in English with a concentration in poetry from UT. Her poems have recently appeared in *Whiskey Island Magazine* and *Yemassee Literary Journal*. She won the poetry award for the 2001 winter/spring issue of *Yemassee* and a graduate poetry prize from UT. She is the assistant editor of *Migrants and Stowaways*.

CURT RODE now teaches English and creative writing at Texas Christian University in Fort Worth, Texas after 13 years of living in Knoxville. His poems have appeared in *Sycamore Review, The Flint Hills Review, Apostrophe,* and *Breathing the Same Air.* He enjoys playing bass guitar when time permits. He also considers himself a master of the catnap.

TEREZ ROSE's writing has appeared in various publications throughout the country, including the *San Jose Mercury-News, The Milwaukee Journal-Sentinel, Peace Corps Online, Big World* travel magazine and in the anthology, *Women Who Eat: A New Generation on the Glory of Food.* She has lived in Central Africa and London but now makes her home with husband and son in Boulder Creek, California. She has recently completed her first novel.

LYNN VEACH SADLER, a former college president in Vermont and native North Carolinian, has published widely in academics and traveled around the world five times. Now a creative writer, she has many publications and awards in fiction, drama, poetry and creative non-fiction. She won *The Pittsburgh Quarterly's* 2001 Hay Prize, tied for first in *Kalliope's* 2002 Elkind Contest, was a runner-up for the 2002 *Spoon River Poetry Review* Editors' Prize Contest and won the Poetry Society of America's 2003 Hemley Award and *Asphodel's* 2003 Poetry Contest.

JANE SASSER's work has appeared in *The Atlanta Review, The North American Review, The National Forum, Sow's Ear, RE:AL, ByLine, The Mid-America Poetry Review, Snowy Egret, Small Pond, The North Carolina Literary Review* and numerous other publications. A high school teacher of English literature, American literature and creative writing, she lives in Oak Ridge, Tennessee.

DEBORAH SCAPEROTH's work has appeared in *New Millennium Writings, Breathing the Same Air, Literary Lunch, Yemassee, Number One* and other literary journals. She lives in Knoxville and is working on her Ph.D. at the University of Tennessee.

PAMELA SCHOENEWALDT lives in Knoxville, where she teaches writing at the University of Tennessee and was Writer in Residence at UT Libraries from 2001-3. She lived in Naples, Italy from 1990-2000. Her short stories have appeared in *Belletrist Review,* Bianco su Nero (Italy), *Carve, Cascando (U.K.), Crescent Review* (winning the Chekhov Prize for Short Fiction), *Iron Horse Literary Review, Mediphors,* Mondogreco, *New Millennium Writings, Literary Lunch, Paris Transcontinental, Pinehurst Journal, Square Lake, The Sun,* and *Women's Words.* Her one-act play in Italian, *"Espresso con Mia Madre,"* was produced at *Teatro Cilea,* Naples. Schoenewaldt's novel in progress is a memoir of a 12th Century Sicilian empress. She lives with her husband, Maurizio, and daughter, Emilia.

TRACY STEINHANDLER SIMMS has published fiction and poetry in literary journals such as *Contrary Magazine, PenEnvy,* and *Imprints,* and her poetry has been awarded Honorable Mentions from the *Red Hen Press 2003 Poetry Award* and *Byline Magazine.* A graduate of Elmhurst College and the University of Chicago, she has studied abroad multiple times, taught composition and literature at various St. Louis colleges and loves to read and write in many genres for various audiences. She lives in Chicago with her husband, Ben, and their two meatball-shaped cats. At the time this went to press, she still isn't sure what she wants to be when she grows up, but she's learning to accept that.

WESLEY SIMS is a native of Lawrence County, Tennessee, and now lives in Oak Ridge with his wife and sons. He works as a computing professional. Besides writing, his hobbies include genealogy, camping and being a soccer parent. He looks forward to retiring and having more time to write, and to looking for a dog suitable for the name OnoMuttoPeia.

SARAH SMALL lives in Alcoa with her husband, a professor of botany at the University of Tennessee, and their three children. She holds a B.A. in English from Milligan College outside of Johnson City, Tennessee and a M.A. in creative writing from Iowa State University. Besides teaching her own three children at home, she teaches creative writing to an enthusiastic and boisterous bunch of elementary and middle-school age kids at Blount County Home Education Association's cooperative.

STEVE SPARKS is originally from North Alabama but has lived in the Knoxville area for the past ten years. He has published poetry in *North American Review, Potpourri, Now & Then, New Millennium Writings* and *Number One*, among others. His work has also previously appeared in the last two Knoxville Writers' Guild anthologies. He has poems forthcoming in the *Sonora Review* and *Northwest Review*.

LAURA STILL is a poet living in Knoxville. She works part-time as a dental practice consultant and USTA certified tennis umpire. Her writing experience includes technical writing for dental education and personnel management, screening poetry for *New Millennium Writings* and screening novels for the Peter Taylor Prize, which is administered jointly by the Knoxville Writers' Guild and UT Press. She is treasurer of the Knoxville Writers' Guild and has administered the Young Writers Poetry Prize since 2002. Her recent publications include *Breathing the Same Air, Literary Lunch,* and *New Millennium Writings.* She has a poem in the upcoming *Christian Guide.* Her other activities include tennis, strength training and writing plays for the children's drama workshop at Church Street United Methodist, where she teaches grades 1 through 5. She also is a graduate of the Actor's Co-op Training Studio, and she participated in the University of Tennessee George Garrett Festival in October 2003 by taking the part of Nag the talking horse in *Sir Slob and the Princess.*

KIM STONE spends most of her time dredging around corporate America. When she gets the chance to travel, she tends to tap into her creative writing roots. She earned a degree in English from Winthrop University in South Carolina where she was published in the annual literary journal, *Anthology*.

LISA SWANSTROM earned a Master's degree in creative writing from the Professional Writing Program at the University of Southern California, where she won an AWP Intro Journals Award for Creative Nonfiction. Her work has appeared in the *Mid-American Review, Closer Magazine* and *Moxie Magazine,* among others. Lisa also co-edits the online literary journal *Sunspinner* and is currently a doctoral candidate in Comparative Literature at the University of California, Santa Barbara.

CATIE TAPPAN is a graduating senior in printmaking at the University of Tennessee. She settled into Knoxville nine years ago, after years of moving around as an "army brat," and has fallen in love with the local history of East Tennessee. Although she loves Knoxville, she is looking forward to traveling to more exotic destinations and continuing her education in the arts.

KIM TREVATHAN is the author of *Paddling the Tennessee River: A Voyage on Easy Water* and is working on a book about his canoe trip down the length of the Cumberland River. He teaches writing and literature at Maryville College.

PATRICIA WATERS was born and reared in Nashville, took her B.A. at Memphis State University, her M.A. and Ph.D. at the University of Tennessee at Knoxville. She has published in little magazines. She was the writer in residence at the University of Tennessee Libraries from 2003-4.

PATRICIA WELLINGHAM-JONES, former psychology researcher, writer, editor, and lecturer, has most recently been published in *Tiger's Eye, Möbius, The Horsethief's Journal, San Gabriel Valley Poetry Quarterly* and *Niederngasse*. She won the Reuben Rose International Poetry Prize (Israel) in 2003.

MELYNDA WHETSEL holds both a Bachelor's and a Master's degree from the University of Tennessee. She has taught introductory art, drawing, painting, printmaking, ceramics, sculpture, photography and advanced art in Knox County Schools for thirty years. She particularly enjoys working in collage and mixed media, as she did for *My Fiftieth Year* which is featured on the cover of this volume. In 2000, Whetsel was nominated as a Tennessee Outstanding Teacher of Humanities. She is also a five-time nominee as a Tennessee Governor's School for the Arts Outstanding Teacher.

JENNY BROOKS WHITE, originally from Tennessee, graduated from Mississippi State University, moved to Japan for a year, then to Ames, Iowa where she recently graduated with a Master's in English specializing in creative writing. Her work has been published by *Kansas English*, accepted at The Des Moines National Poetry Festival and most recently at the Southern Writers, Southern Writing Conference in Oxford, Mississippi. She currently lives and teaches in Jackson, Tennessee.

KELLEY JEAN WHITE is a mother of three, a Quaker, an inner city pediatrician for more than twenty years, a collector of stray animals and a seeker after Buddha nature. She has published two full length poetry collections, *The Patient Presents* and *Late*; two chapbooks, *I am going to walk toward the sanctuary* and *Against Medical Advice* with more forthcoming.

TISH WHITE, having raised four children, is currently a student at University of Tennessee pursuing an undergraduate degree in creative writing. She credits any development of talent she may have for poetry writing to Dr. Jo Angela Edwins who taught her about the possible layers of meaning a writer could obtain in concrete imagery.

DON WILLIAMS is a short story writer, founding editor of *New Millennium Writings* (an annual anthology of prose and poetry) and a columnist and former feature writer for *The Knoxville News-Sentinel*, where his honors include a Malcolm Law Award, a Sigma Delta Chi Golden Presscard, several Scripps Howard awards and a NEH Journalism Fellowship at the University of Michigan. His short stories and articles have been anthologized. He is a founding member of the Knoxville Writers' Guild and directs the Leslie Garrett Fiction Prize. His just finished novel, *Oracle of the Orchid Lounge*, is in search of a publisher.

BOB R. WILSON was born in LaFollette, Tennessee in 1954 where he currently resides. In 1986, he received an art degree from Berea College. Both his art and his poetry have been published in the following local publications: *Bellicose Lettres*, *Poetry for Breakfast*, *A-1 Lab Dispenser*, *Medium* and *Knoxville Brew*. He has been a member of both the Chroma Artists' Association and A-1 in Knoxville.

_I_NDEX OF CONTRIBUTORS

*I*NDEX OF CONTRIBUTORS

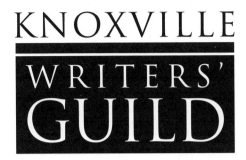

KNOXVILLE
WRITERS'
GUILD

OFFICERS AND BOARD
2004

PRESIDENT
Ed Sullivan

VICE PRESIDENT
Kay Newton

SECRETARY
Pamela Schoenewaldt

TREASURER
Laura Still

Tony Day
Judy DiGregorio
Emily Dziuban
David E. Joyner
J. Brian Long
Robert Lydick
Dennis McCarthy
Kristin Robertson
Inga Treitler
Nicole Underwood